Secrets Mormons DON'T Want YOU To Know

Richard & Cindy Benson

CHICK PUBLICATIONS

For a complete list of distributors near you,
call (909) 987-0771, or visit **www.chick.com**

Copyright ©2011 by Richard and Cindy Benson

Published by:
 CHICK PUBLICATIONS
 PO Box 3500, Ontario, Calif. 91761-1019 USA
 Tel: (909) 987-0771
 Fax: (909) 941-8128
 Web: www.chick.com
 Email: postmaster@chick.com

Printed in the United States of America

First Printing

Quotes Bruce R. McConkie's book *Mormon Doctrine* are from the 1966 edition unless otherwise noted.

All rights reserved. No part of this book may be reproduced, stored in a retrieval system or transmitted in any form or by any means (electronic, mechanical, photocopying, recording or otherwise) without permission in writing from the copyright owner.

ISBN: 978-07589-0785-1

ABOUT THE MORMONS QUOTED IN THIS BOOK

Joseph Smith – The founder and first president of the Mormon church.

Brigham Young – The second President of the Mormon church, from December 27, 1847 until his death on August 29, 1877. He was the founder of Salt Lake City and the first governor of the Utah Territory. Brigham Young University was named in his honor.

Orson Pratt – (1811-1881) He was an original member of the Quorum of Twelve Apostles.

John Taylor – The third President of the Mormon church, from October 10, 1880 to July 25, 1887.

Bruce McConkie – A member of the First Council of the Seventy of the LDS Church from 1946 until his calling to the Quorum of the Twelve Apostles in 1972, where he served until his death in 1985. He published several doctrinal books and articles.

Joseph Fielding Smith – (1876-1972). The tenth president of the LDS church. He was the son of Joseph F. Smith, the sixth president. His grandfather, Hyrum Smith, was the brother of Church founder Joseph Smith, Jr. He was President of the Quorum of the Twelve Apostles for 19 years (1951-1970), and was a religious scholar and a prolific writer. Many of his works are used as references for church members.

CONTENTS

About the Mormons quoted in the book 3
Introduction 7
Who is God? 9
Jesus Christ 29
The Holy Spirit 42
Salvation 44
Blood atonement 51
The Bible 54
The Book of Mormon 56
Mormon church: only way to heaven 59
Joseph Smith 61
Joseph Smith's false prophecies 79
Black people 87
Good works redeem the dead 95
Baptism 96
Adam 102
Lucifer 106
Hell 108

Temple garments	112
Bizarre teachings of Brigham Young	113
Sins that deserve instant death	118
Polygamy	121
Marriage for eternity	125
Mormonism's ever-changing name	126
The Masonry connection	127
Mormon prophets	130
Do Mormon leaders hate Christianity?	133
Mormon temples	135
Mormon contradictions	136
The spirit world	139
Mormon teachings about man	142
More strange Mormon teachings	144
Why we left the Mormon church	158
Summary of what Mormons believe	199
Are Mormons encouraged to lie?	203
Conclusion	205

INTRODUCTION

When I was an 11-year-old girl, I received the shock of my life.

I had been born and raised in a Mormon home and I felt that made me special. I was always thankful to God for that privilege. My life-long goal was to go on a Mormon mission, get married to a wonderful Mormon man, bear children, then live forever in our celestial kingdom as a goddess along with my eternal husband.

But all those dreams began to unravel the day my 53-year-old father brought home a 15-year-old girl and told us he had to take her as his second wife in order to fulfill the law of eternal progression towards his own godhood.

One day we were a happy family, and the next day devastation struck—and my life was sent spiraling.

Later in the book I'll tell you the whole story but first I want you to see some secrets about the Mormon religion that Mormons really don't want you to know.

I pray that you will be blessed.

> In Christ's love,
> Cindy Benson

WHO IS GOD?

Secret 1

Mormonism denies the Trinity:

"Three glorified, exalted, and perfected personages comprise the Godhead or supreme presidency of the universe... They are: God the Father; God the Son; God the Holy Ghost... each God in the Godhead is a personage, separate and distinct from each of the others...Each occupies space and is and can be in but one place at one time..."[1]

Joseph Smith said:

"All are to be crammed into one God, according to sectarianism. It would make the biggest God in all the world. He would be a wonderfully big God—he would be a giant or a monster."[2]

Bruce McConkie added:

"Three separate personages—Father, Son, and Holy Ghost—comprise the Godhead. As each of these persons is a God, it is evident, from this standpoint alone, that a plurality of Gods exist."[3]

---

1) Bruce R. McConkie, *Mormon Doctrine*, p. 319.
2) Joseph Fielding Smith, *Teachings of the Prophet Joseph Smith,* p. 372.
3) McConkie, *Mormon Doctrine,* p. 576.

"There are three Gods—the Father, Son, and Holy Ghost…"[4]

Joseph Fielding Smith agreed:

"I have always declared God to be a distinct personage, Jesus Christ a separate and distinct personage from God the Father, and that the Holy Ghost was a distinct personage and a Spirit: and these three constitute three distinct personages and three Gods… I have it from God, and get over it if you can."[5]

What the Bible says:

"For there are three that bear record in heaven, the Father, the Word, and the Holy Ghost: and these three are one." (1 John 5:7)

See also Genesis 1:26; 11:7, Isaiah 6:8, Matthew 28:19.

Secret 2

Mormonism says God used to be a man on another planet:

"God used to be a man on another planet…"[6]

What the Bible says:

"Before the mountains were brought forth, or ever thou hadst formed the earth and the world, even from everlasting to everlasting, thou art God." (Psalm 90:2)

---

4) McConkie, *Mormon Doctrine*, p. 317.
5) Smith, *Teachings of the Prophet Joseph Smith*, pp. 370-371.
6) McConkie, *Mormon Doctrine*, p. 321; Joseph Smith, *Times and Seasons*, vol. 5, pp. 613-614; *Journal of Discourses*, vol. 2, p. 345, and vol. 7, p. 333.

Secret 3

Mormonism says that God the Father also had a father:

"If Jesus Christ was the Son of God, and John discovered that God the Father of Jesus Christ had a Father, you may suppose that He had a Father also. Where was there ever a son without a father? And where was there ever a father without first being a son?" [7]

What the Bible says:

"…before me there was no God formed, neither shall there be after me." (Isaiah 43:10)

Secret 4

Mormon doctrine says there are many Gods:

Brigham Young taught that the number of Gods is uncountable. [8]

"…there is an infinite number of holy personages, drawn from worlds without number, who have passed on to exaltation and are thus gods." [9]

"…you have got to learn how to be Gods yourselves… the same as all Gods have done before you." [10]

Joseph Smith said:

"Hence, the doctrine of a plurality of Gods

---

7) Joseph Smith, *History of the Church*, vol. 6, pp. 473-479.
8) John A. Widtsoe, *Discourses of Brigham Young*, p. 22.
9) McConkie, *Mormon Doctrine*, pp. 576-577.
10) Smith, *Teachings of the Prophet Joseph Smith*, p. 346.

is as prominent in the Bible as any other doctrine. It is all over the face of the Bible. It stands beyond the power of controversy.[11]

"In the beginning, the head of the Gods called a council of the Gods; and they came together and concocted a plan to create the world and people it."[12]

"If we should take a million of worlds like this and number their particles, we should find that there are more Gods than there are particles of matter in those worlds."[13]

"The Gods who dwell in Heaven... have been redeemed from the grave in a world which existed before the foundations of this earth were laid... They were exalted also, from fallen men to Celestial Gods to inhabit their Heaven forever and ever."[14]

"The celestial beings who dwell in the Heaven... having been filled with all the fulness of these eternal attributes, are called Gods, because the fulness of God dwells in each. Both the males and the females enjoy this fulness."[15]

What the Bible says:

"Look unto me, and be ye saved, all the ends

---

11) Smith, *History of the Church*, vol. 6, pp. 473-479.
12) *Journal of Discourses*, vol. 6, p. 5.
13) Ibid., vol. 2, p. 345.
14) Orson Pratt, *The Seer*, p. 23.
15) Pratt, *The Seer,* p. 37.

of the earth: for I am God, and there is none else." (Isaiah 45:22)

See Deuteronomy 4:35; 6:4, Psalm 86:10, Isaiah 43:10-11; 44:6,8; 45:5-6,18,21; 46:9, Mark 12:29, 32, 1 Corinthians 8:4-6, 1 Timothy 2:5, 1 John 5:7.

Secret 5

Mormons believe that men can become Gods:

"As man is, God once was, as God is, man may become." [16]

"...that man is the offspring of God... having within him the seeds of godhood and thus being a god in embryo..." [17]

"The Lord created you and me for the purpose of becoming Gods like Himself...We are created... to become Gods..." [18]

"...you have got to learn how to be Gods yourselves..." [19]

"...man is the king of kings and the lord of lords in embryo." [20]

"Each one of you has it within the realm of his possibility to develop a kingdom over which you will reside as its king and god." [21]

"To know God, we must know ourselves. All

---
16) Lorenzo Snow, *Millennial Star,* vol. 54, p. 404.
17) Spencer W. Kimball, *The Miracle of Forgiveness,* p. 3.
18) *Journal of Discourses*, vol. 3, p. 93.
19) Smith, *Teachings of the Prophet Joseph Smith,* p. 346.
20) *Journal of Discourses*, vol. 10, p. 223.
21) Spencer W. Kimball, *Teachings of Spencer W. Kimball,* p. 31.

the personal attributes which are ascribed to God... we find in ourselves... Mormonism does not tend to debase God to the level of man, but to exalt man to the perfection of God."[22]

"Each command we obey sends us another rung up the ladder to perfected manhood and toward godhood; and every law disobeyed is a sliding toward the bottom where man merges into the brute world."[23]

What the Bible says:

"And I heard a great voice out of heaven saying, Behold, the tabernacle of God is with men, and he will dwell with them, and they shall be his people, and God himself shall be with them, and be their God." (Revelation 21:3)

See also Revelation 20:6.

Secret 6

Mormonism says we have to learn how to be Gods:

"Here, then, is eternal life—to know the only wise and true God; and you have got to learn how to be Gods yourselves, and to be kings and priests to God, the same as all Gods have done before you, namely, by going from one small degree to another, and from a small capacity to a great one; from

---

22) Charles W. Penrose, Millennial Star, vol. 23, p. 180.
23) Kimball, *Teachings of Spencer W. Kimball*, p. 153.

grace to grace, from exaltation to exaltation, until you attain to the resurrection of the dead, and are able to dwell in everlasting burnings, and to sit in glory, as do those who sit enthroned in everlasting power."[24]

What the Bible says:

Thus saith the LORD the King of Israel, and his redeemer the LORD of hosts; I am the first, and I am the last; and beside me there is no God. (Isaiah 44:6)

Secret 7

Mormonism teaches that God was once a man:

"We have imagined and supposed that God was God from all eternity. I will now refute that idea, and take away the veil, so that you may see… he was once a man like us…"[25]

"Remember that God, our heavenly Father, was perhaps once a child, and mortal like we ourselves, and rose step by step in the scale of progress, in the school of advancement; has moved forward and overcome, until He has arrived at the point where He now is."[26]

"Mormon prophets have continuously taught the sublime truth that God the Eternal Father was once a mortal man who passed through a school of earth life similar to that

---

24) Smith, *Teachings of the Prophet Joseph Smith,* pp. 346-347.
25) Ibid., pp. 345-346.
26) *Journal of Discourses,* vol. 1, p. 123.

through which we are now passing. He became God—an exalted being—through obedience to the same eternal Gospel truths that we are given opportunity today to obey... Thus He grew in experience and continued to grow until He attained the status of Godhood. In other words, He became God by absolute obedience to all the eternal laws of the Gospel..."[27]

What the Bible says:

"Before the mountains were brought forth, or ever thou hadst formed the earth and the world, even from everlasting to everlasting, thou art God." (Psalm 90:2)

See also Habakkuk 1:12, Hebrews 13:8, Psalm 93:2, Revelation 1:8.

Secret 8

Mormon doctrine says that God is an exalted man:

"God himself was once as we are now, and is an exalted man, and sits enthroned in yonder heavens... he was once a man like us; yea, that God himself, the Father of us all, dwelt on an earth, the same as Jesus Christ himself did; and I will show it from the Bible... The Scriptures say it, and I defy all the learning and wisdom and all the combined powers of earth and hell together to refute it."[28]

---

27) Milton R. Hunter, *The Gospel Through the Ages,* pp. 104, 115.
28) Smith, *Teachings of the Prophet Joseph Smith,* pp. 345-346.

"God himself, the Father of us all, is a glorified, exalted, immortal, resurrected Man!" [29]

"He is our Father—the Father of our spirits, and was once a man in mortal flesh as we are and is now an exalted Being." [30]

"GOD IS AN EXALTED MAN... our Father in heaven at one time passed through a life and death and is an exalted man." [31]

"What man is, God has been and what God is, man seeks to become." [32]

"False creeds teach that God is a spirit essence that fills the immensity of space and is everywhere and nowhere in particular present... God the Father is a glorified and perfected Man, a Personage of flesh and bones..." [33]

What the Bible says:

"...for I am God, and not man..." (Hosea 11:9)

See 1 Samuel 15:29, Romans 1:22-23.

Secret 9

Mormonism says a man became God by obeying Gospel truths:

"Remember that God, our heavenly Father, was perhaps once a child, and mortal like we ourselves, and rose step by step in the scale of progress, in the school of advancement; has

---

29) McConkie, *Mormon Doctrine*, p. 643.
30) *Journal of Discourses*, vol. 7, p. 333.
31) Joseph Fielding Smith, *Doctrines of Salvation*, vol. 1, p. 10.
32) Spencer W. Kimball, Salt Lake Tribune, April 3, 1977.
33) McConkie, *Mormon Doctrine*, pp. 318-319.

moved forward and overcome, until He has arrived at the point where He now is."[34]

"Mormon prophets have continuously taught the sublime truth that God the Eternal Father was once a mortal man who passed through a school of earth life similar to that through which we are now passing. He became God—an exalted being—through obedience to the same eternal Gospel truths that we are given opportunity today to obey... Thus He grew in experience and continued to grow until He attained the status of Godhood... He became God by absolute obedience to all the eternal laws of the Gospel..."[35]

What the Bible says:
"God is not a man, that he should lie; neither the son of man, that he should repent: hath he said, and shall he not do it? or hath he spoken, and shall he not make it good?" (Numbers 23:19)

Secret 10

Mormonism teaches that men and women who become Gods will have children throughout eternity:

"...the Gods were to be parents of spirit children just as our Heavenly Father and Heavenly Mother were the parents of the people of this earth."[36]

---
34) *Journal of Discourses*, vol. 1, p. 123.
35) Hunter, *The Gospel Through the Ages*, pp. 104, 115.
36) Ibid., p. 120.

"Mortal persons who overcome all things and gain an ultimate exaltation will live eternally in the family unit and have spirit children, thus becoming Eternal Fathers and Eternal Mothers... Godhood is not for men only; it is for men and women together."[37]

"In the Heaven where our spirits were born, there are many Gods, each of whom has his own wife or wives... Each God, through his wife or wives, raises up a numerous family of sons and daughters... for each father and mother will be in a condition to multiply forever and ever.

"As soon as each God has begotten many millions of male and female spirits, and his Heavenly inheritance becomes too small, to comfortably accommodate his great family, he, in connection with his sons, organizes a new world... where he sends both male and female spirits to inhabit tabernacles of flesh and bones...

If the Father of these spirits... had secured to himself, through the everlasting covenant of marriage, many wives... the period required to people a world would be shorter... in proportion to the number of wives... if it required one hundred thousand million of years to people a world like this... it is evident

---

37) McConkie, *Mormon Doctrine*, pp. 517, 844.

that, with a hundred wives, this period would be reduced to only one thousand million years."[38]

What the Bible says:

"And as it is appointed unto men once to die, but after this the judgment:" (Hebrews 9:27)

Secret 11

Mormonism says God lives on a planet near a star called Kolob:

"And I saw the stars, that they were very great, and that one of them was nearest unto the throne of God... and the name of the great one is Kolob, because it is near unto me, for I am the Lord thy God..."

And thus there shall be the reckoning of the time of one planet above another, until thou come nigh unto Kolob, which Kolob is after the reckoning of the Lord's time; which Kolob is set nigh unto the throne of God..."[39]

What the Bible says:

"...Our Father which art in heaven, Hallowed be thy name." (Matthew 6:9)

Secret 12

Mormonism teaches that God can only form and organize existing matter. He can't create:

"To create is to organize. It is an utterly false

---

38) Pratt, *The Seer*, pp. 37, 39.
39) Pearl of Great Price, Abraham 3:2-3, 9.

Secrets Mormons Don't Want You To Know

and uninspired notion to believe that the world or any other thing was created out of nothing..."[40]

"And then the Lord said: Let us go down. And they went down at the beginning, and they, that is the Gods, organized and formed the heavens and the earth."[41]

"In the beginning the head of the Gods brought forth the Gods... The head of the Gods called the Gods together. I want to show a little learning as well as other fools. The head God organized the heavens and the earth. I defy all the world to refute me. In the beginning the heads of the Gods organized the heavens and the earth."[42]

What the Bible says:
"Where wast thou when I laid the foundations of the earth? declare, if thou hast understanding." (Job 38:4)

See Genesis 1:1, John 1:1,3,10, Psalm 148:5, Isaiah 42:5, Hebrews 11:3.

Secret 13

Mormonism teaches that God did not have the power to create the spirit of man.

"...I might with boldness proclaim from the

---
40) McConkie, *Mormon Doctrine*, p. 169.
41) Pearl of Great Price, Abraham 4:1.
42) Smith, *Teachings of the Prophet Joseph Smith,* pp. 371-372.

house-tops that God never had the power to create the spirit of man at all. God himself could not create himself."[43]

What the Bible says:

"And the LORD God formed man of the dust of the ground, and breathed into his nostrils the breath of life; and man became a living soul." (Genesis 2:7)

See also Genesis 1:27, 18:14, Job 42:2, Matthew 28:18.

Secret 14

Mormonism teaches that there is both an Eternal Father and an Eternal Mother Deity in heaven:

"Implicit in the Christian verity that all men are the spirit children of an Eternal Father is the usually unspoken truth that they are also the offspring of an Eternal Mother. An exalted and glorified Man of Holiness (Moses 6:57) could not be a Father unless a Woman of like glory, perfection, and holiness was associated with him as a Mother... This doctrine that there is a Mother in Heaven was affirmed in plainness by the First Presidency of the Church (Joseph F. Smith, John R. Winder, and Anthon H. Lund) when, in speaking of pre-existence and the origin of man, they said that 'man, as a spirit, was begotten and born of heavenly parents, and

---

[43] Smith, *Teachings of the Prophet Joseph Smith*, p. 354.

reared to maturity in the eternal mansions of the Father,' that man is the 'offspring of celestial parentage,' and that 'all men and women are in the similitude of the universal Father and Mother, and are literally the sons and daughters of Deity.'"[44]

"...the Gods were to be parents of spirit children just as our Heavenly Father and Heavenly Mother were the parents of the people of this earth."[45]

"I think the revelations which Jesus Christ gave through the Prophet Joseph Smith concerning motherhood are the greatest contribution the world has ever received on this subject; for it was, so far as I know, never taught before in the history of the world that not only have we a Father in Heaven but we have a Mother there also. No matter to what heights God has attained or may attain, He does not stand alone; for side by side with Him, in all Her glory, a glory like unto His, stands a companion, the Mother of His children. For as we have a Father in Heaven, so also we have a Mother there, a glorified, exalted, ennobled Mother."[46]

---

44) McConkie, *Mormon Doctrine*, p. 516.
45) Hunter, *The Gospel Through the Ages*, p. 120.
46) Dr. Douglas E. Brinley, Professor of Church History at BYU, from his address entitled "The Importance of Fathers and Mothers," given at the 2001 BYU Families Under Fire Conference.

What the Bible says:
> "...the LORD he is God in heaven above, and upon the earth beneath: there is none else." (Deuteronomy 4:39)

The only reference to a female goddess in the Bible is in heathen, idolatrous worship.

Secret 15

Mormon doctrine says God is imperfect and always changing:

> "God himself is increasing and progressing in knowledge, power, and dominion, and will do so, worlds without end."[47]

> "...the God that I serve is progressing eternally."[48]

> "We believe in a God who is Himself progressive...whose perfection consists in eternal advancement—a Being who has attained His exalted state by a path which now His children are permitted to follow... In spite of the opposition of the sects, in the face of direct charges of blasphemy, the Church proclaims the eternal truth: 'As man is, God once was; as God is, man may be.'"[49]

What the Bible says:
> "As for God, his way is perfect..." (Psalm 18:30)

See also Malachi 3:6, Psalm 102:26-27.

---

47) *Journal of Discourses*, vol. 6, p. 120.
48) Ibid., vol. 11, p. 286.
49) James E. Talmage, *Articles of Faith*, p. 430.

Secret 16

Mormonism says God and Jesus have bodies of flesh and bone:

"The Father has a body of flesh and bones as tangible as man's; the Son also; but the Holy Ghost has not a body of flesh and bones, but is a personage of Spirit. Were it not so, the Holy Ghost could not dwell in us."[50]

"False creeds teach that God is a spirit essence that fills the immensity of space and is everywhere and nowhere in particular present... God the Father is a glorified and perfected Man, a Personage of flesh and bones..."[51]

Brigham Young said, "If our Father and God should be disposed to walk through these aisles, we should not know Him from one of the congregation. You would see a man and that is all you would know about Him."[52]

What the Bible says:
"God is a Spirit..." (John 4:24)

Secret 17

Mormon doctrine says God is NOT omnipresent:

"False creeds teach that God is a Spirit essence that fills the immensity of space and is everywhere and nowhere in particular present."[53]

---

50) Doctrine and Covenants 130:22-23.
51) McConkie, *Mormon Doctrine*, pp. 318-319.
52) *Journal of Discourses*, vol. 2, p. 40.
53) McConkie, *Mormon Doctrine*, p. 318.

> "It has been said, therefore, that God is everywhere present; but this does not mean that the actual person of any one member of the Godhead can be physically present in more than one place at one time… His person cannot be in more than one place at any one time… It is impossible for Him to occupy at one time more than one space of such limits…"[54]

> "Every one knows that it is absurd to believe in a personage being present in two places at once… there are things which are impossible with God… He could not place His body in Europe and America at the same time… Those who are called the wisest among the religious world have made it out, that the persons of the Father and Son can be in them and in every other place at the same instant of time. This is as gross an absurdity as it would be to say that three times three make ten…"[55]

What the Bible says:

> "For where two or three are gathered together in my name, there am I in the midst of them." (Matthew 18:20)

See also Psalm 139:7-10, Proverbs 5:21; 15:3, Jeremiah 23:23-24.

---

54) Talmage, *Articles of Faith,* p. 43.
55) *Journal of Discourses,* vol. 2, pp. 343-344.

Secret 18

Mormonism teaches that God is married, and a polygamist:

"We have now clearly shown that God the Father had a plurality of wives, one or more being in eternity... We have also proved that both God the Father and our Lord Jesus Christ inherit their wives in eternity as well as in time..."[56]

"All men and women are in the similitude of the universal Father and Mother, and are literally the sons and daughters of Deity; as spirits they were the offspring of celestial parentage."[57]

"...plural marriage is the patriarchal order of marriage lived by God and others who reign in the Celestial Kingdom."[58]

What the Bible says:

The Bible teaches that God is a Spirit—and Spirits don't get married or have children.

Secret 19

Mormon doctrine says God commanded Abraham to have his wife lie:

"...the Lord said unto me... therefore see that ye do on this wise: Let her say unto the Egyptians, she is thy sister..."[59]

---

56) Pratt, *The Seer*, p. 172.
57) McConkie, *Mormon Doctrine*, p. 589.
58) John J. Stewart, *Brigham Young and His Wives*, p. 41.
59) Pearl of Great Price, Abraham 2:22-24.

What the Bible says:
> "These six things doth the LORD hate: yea, seven are an abomination unto him... a lying tongue..." (Proverbs 6:16-17)

Secret 20

Mormonism teaches that Mary was God's wife:

Mormon doctrine claims that all human beings born on earth are the spirit children of Elohim and one of his wives."[60] At the appointed time, the god of Mormonism supposedly came to visit Mary, and they had a physical relationship and conceived the child Jesus.[61]

This would make the god of Mormonism guilty of committing incest with Mary because, according to some Mormon sources, she is his daughter.

According to other Mormon sources, Mary is the wife of Elohim.[62] Therefore, Mary would be guilty of committing incest with Joseph because he would be her spiritual son or stepson, depending on which mother-goddess he was born to.

Either way, it is a horrible, ungodly mess. Mormon Apostle Orson Pratt taught:

> "The fleshly body of Jesus required a Mother as well as a Father. Therefore, the Father and

---
60) Hunter, *Gospel Through the Ages,* p. 120; Pratt, *The Seer,* p. 172; McConkie, *Mormon Doctrine,* p. 750-751.
61) McConkie, *Mormon Doctrine,* pp. 547, 742; *Journal of Discourses,* vol. 8, p. 115.
62) Pratt, *The Seer,* p. 158.

Mother of Jesus, according to the flesh, must have been associated together in the capacity of Husband and Wife; hence the Virgin Mary must have been, for the time being, the lawful wife of God the Father:"[63]

What the Bible says:
"But while he [Joseph] thought on these things, behold, the angel of the Lord appeared unto him in a dream, saying, Joseph, thou son of David, fear not to take unto thee Mary thy wife: for that which is conceived in her is of the Holy Ghost." (Matthew 1:20)

JESUS CHRIST

Secret 21
Mormons believe it's wrong to worship Jesus Christ:
"We worship the Father and him only and no one else. We do not worship the Son, and we do not worship the Holy Ghost."[64]

What the Bible says:
"…when he bringeth in the firstbegotten (Jesus Christ) into the world, he saith, And let all the angels of God worship him." (Hebrews 1:6)

---
63) Pratt, *The Seer*, p. 158.
64) Devotional address at Brigham Young University by Bruce R. McConkie on March 2, 1982. http://speeches.byu.edu/reader/reader.php?id=6843

Secret 22

Mormonism teaches that Jesus Christ was NOT begotten by the Holy Ghost:

> "Now, remember from this time forth, and for ever, that Jesus Christ was *not* begotten by the Holy Ghost." [65]

> "The birth of the Saviour was as natural as are the births of our children; it was the result of natural action. He partook of flesh and blood—was begotten of his Father, as we were of our fathers." [66]

> "Christ was begotten of God. He was not born without the aid of Man, and that Man was God!" [67]

> "They tell us the Book of Mormon states that Jesus was begotten of the Holy Ghost. I challenge the statement. The Book of Mormon teaches no such thing! Neither does the Bible." [68]

In this last quote, Joseph Fielding Smith insists that the Book of Mormon does NOT state that Jesus was begotten of the Holy Ghost. Read it for yourself and decide:

> "… she [Mary] being a virgin, a precious and chosen vessel, who shall be overshadowed and

---

[65] *Journal of Discourses*, vol. 1, p. 51.
[66] Ibid., vol. 8, p. 115.
[67] Smith, *Doctrines of Salvation*, vol. 1, p. 18.
[68] Ibid., p. 19.

conceive by the power of the Holy Ghost, and bring forth a son, yea, even the Son of God."[69]

What the Bible says:

"...When as his mother Mary was espoused to Joseph, before they came together, she was found with child of the Holy Ghost." (Matthew 1:18)

"Behold, a virgin shall be with child, and shall bring forth a son, and they shall call his name Emmanuel, which being interpreted is, God with us." (Matthew 1:23)

Secret 23

Mormon doctrine says Christ does NOT live in your heart:

"...the idea that the Father and the Son dwell in a man's heart is an old sectarian notion, and is false."[70]

What the Bible says:

"That Christ may dwell in your hearts by faith..." (Ephesians 3:17)

Secret 24

Mormonism teaches that Jesus had to be baptized to gain admission to the celestial kingdom:

"1. He humbled himself before the Father; 2. He covenanted to be obedient and keep the Father's commandments; 3. He had to

---

69) Book of Mormon, Alma 7:10.
70) Doctrine and Covenants 130:3.

be baptized to gain admission to the celestial kingdom; and 4. He set an example for all men to follow."[71]

What the Bible says:

Jesus Christ, as part of the Trinity, created heaven. To say He had to be baptized to gain admittance is to strip Him of His deity.

> "For by him (Jesus Christ) were all things created, that are in heaven, and that are in earth, visible and invisible, whether they be thrones, or dominions, or principalities, or powers: all things were created by him, and for him:" (Colossians 1:16)

Secret 25

Mormonism teaches that after Jesus' resurrection, He visited the people of the Americas:

> "...there were a great multitude gathered together, of the people of Nephi, round about the temple which was in the land Bountiful [somewhere in the Americas]; And... they heard a voice as if it came out of heaven... And... it said unto them: Behold my Beloved Son, in whom I am well pleased...
>
> "And... they saw a Man descending out of heaven; and he was clothed in a white robe; and he came down and stood in the midst of them... And... he stretched forth his hand and

---

71) McConkie, *Mormon Doctrine*, p. 71.

spake unto the people, saying: Behold, I am Jesus Christ... And it came to pass that when Jesus had spoken these words the whole multitude fell to the earth; for they remembered that it had been prophesied among them that Christ should show himself unto them after his ascension into heaven."[72]

What the Bible says:
The Bible says absolutely nothing about this.

Secret 26

Mormon doctrine says God the Father, Jesus Christ, and the Holy Spirit are three separate and distinct personages:

"Three glorified, exalted, and perfected personages comprise the Godhead or supreme presidency of the universe... They are: God the Father; God the Son; God the Holy Ghost... each God in the Godhead is a personage, separate and distinct from each of the others... Each occupies space and is and can be in but one place at one time..."[73]

"Everlasting covenant was made between three personages before the organization of this earth, and relates to their dispensation of things to men on the earth..."[74]

---

72) 3 Nephi 11:1,3,5,7,8,9,10,12.
73) McConkie, *Mormon Doctrine*, p. 319.
74) Smith, *Teachings of the Prophet Joseph Smith*, p. 190.

What the Bible says:
> "For there are three that bear record in heaven, the Father, the Word, and the Holy Ghost: and these three are one." (1 John 5:7)

Secret 27

Mormonism says Jesus was born in Jerusalem:
> "And behold, he shall be born of Mary, at Jerusalem..."[75]

What the Bible says:
> "Now when Jesus was born in Bethlehem of Judaea..." (Matthew 2:1)

See also Micah 5:2, Luke 2:4.

Secret 28

Early Mormon leaders taught that Jesus was conceived when God the Father had literal sex with Mary:
> "...how are children begotten? I answer just as Jesus Christ was begotten of his father... We must come down to the simple fact that God Almighty was the Father of His Son Jesus Christ. Mary, the virgin girl, who had never known mortal man, was his mother. God by her begot His son Jesus Christ..."[76]

Brigham Young declared:

> When the Virgin Mary conceived the child

---

75) Book of Mormon, Alma 7:10.
76) Family Home Evening, 1972, pp. 125-126. Quoted from Mormon website: www.4mormon.org/mormon-Jesus-begotten.php

Secrets Mormons Don't Want You To Know

Jesus, the Father had begotten him in his own likeness. He was not begotten by the Holy Ghost."[77]

Apostle Orson Pratt adds:

"The fleshly body of Jesus required a Mother as well as a Father. Therefore, the Father and Mother of Jesus, according to the flesh, must have been associated in the capacity of husband and wife; hence the Virgin Mary must have been, for the time being, the lawful wife of God the Father... "He had a lawful right to overshadow the Virgin Mary IN THE CAPACITY OF A HUSBAND, and beget a Son...

"Whether God the Father gave Mary to Joseph for time only, or for time and eternity, we are not informed. It may be that He only gave her to be the wife of Joseph while in this mortal state, and that He intended after the resurrection to again take her as one of his own wives to raise up immortal spirits in eternity."[78]

"He created man, as we create our children; for there is no other process of creation..."[79]

What the Bible says:

"...a virgin shall conceive, and bear a son, and shall call his name Immanuel." (Isaiah 7:14)

See also Matthew 1:18, 23, Luke 1:26-35.

---

77) *Journal of Discourses*, vol. 1, pp. 50-51.
78) Pratt, *The Seer*, p. 158.
79) *Journal of Discourses*, vol. 11, p. 122.

Secret 29

Mormon doctrine says that Jesus was married:

From the *Journal of Discourses* we read:

> "...Jesus Christ was married at Cana of Galilee..."[80]

> "...some of the Eastern papers represent me as a great blasphemer, because I said, in my lecture on Marriage, at our last Conference, that Jesus Christ was married at Cana of Galilee, that Mary, Martha, and others were his wives, and that he begat children."[81]

> "...there was a marriage in Cana of Galilee; and... no less a person than Jesus Christ was married on that occasion. If he was never married, his intimacy with Mary and Martha, and the other Mary also whom Jesus loved, must have been highly unbecoming and improper to say the best of it."[82]

> "...Jesus was the bridegroom at the marriage of Cana of Galilee, and he told them what to do... We say it was Jesus Christ who was married, to be brought into the relation whereby he could see his seed, before he was crucified."[83]

While such notions were taught openly during the

---

80) *Journal of Discourses*, vol. 2, p. 210.
81) Ibid.
82) Ibid., vol. 4, p. 259.
83) Ibid., vol. 2, p. 82.

Secrets Mormons Don't Want You To Know 37

presidencies of Joseph Smith and Brigham Young, the current membership is cautioned not to throw such spiritual pearls before scoffing swine.[84]

What the Bible says:

Jesus was *invited* to the wedding (John 2:2). People are not *invited* to their own wedding.

Secret 30

Mormonism says Jesus Christ was a polygamist and a father:

"...the great Messiah who was the founder of the Christian religion, was a Polygamist... the Messiah chose to take upon himself his seed; and by marrying many honorable wives himself, show to all future generations that he approbated the plurality of Wives..."[85]

"We have also proved most clearly that the Son followed the example of his Father, and became the great Bridegroom to whom kings' daughters and many honorable Wives to be married."[86]

"...Jesus Christ was married at Cana of Galilee, that Mary, Martha, and others were his wives, and that he begat children."[87]

What the Bible says:

The Bible simply does not teach this.

---

84) *Journal of Discourses*, vol. 2. p. 210; vol. 4. pp. 259-260; vol. 1, p. 346.
85) Pratt, *The Seer*, p. 172.
86) Ibid.
87) *Journal of Discourses*, vol. 2, p. 210.

Secret 31

Mormon doctrine says Christ was persecuted and crucified because he believed in polygamy:

"The grand reason of the burst of public sentiment in anathemas upon Christ and his disciples, causing his crucifixion, was evidently based upon polygamy... A belief in the doctrine of a plurality of wives caused the persecution of Jesus and his followers. We might almost think they were 'Mormons'. [88]

What the Bible says:

"...Christ died for our sins according to the scriptures;" (1 Corinthians 15:3)

Secret 32

Mormonism says Jesus Christ cannot save:

"The world should know that since the Lord himself cannot save men in their sins..." [89]

"...Therefore, ye cannot be saved in your sins." [90]

"We believe that through the Atonement of Christ, all mankind may be saved, by obedience to the laws and ordinances of the Gospel." [91]

"...we are the only people that know how to save our progenitors, how to save ourselves,

---

88) *Journal of Discourses,* vol. 1, p. 346.
89) Kimball, *The Miracle of Forgiveness,* p. 167.
90) Book of Mormon, Alma 11:37.
91) Articles of Faith #3.

and how to save our posterity... we in fact are the saviors of the world..."[92]

What the Bible says:
"Neither is there salvation in any other: for there is none other name under heaven given among men, whereby we must be saved." (Acts 4:12)

See also Matthew 1:21, Luke 2:11; 19:10, Acts 16:30-31, Jude 25, John 3:17; 14:6, Hebrews 7:25.

Secret 33

Mormon doctrine teaches that Jesus Christ is one of many Gods, and earned His way into Godhood.

"Jesus became a God and reached His great state of understanding through consistent effort and continuous obedience to all the Gospel truths and universal laws."[93]

"As far as man is concerned, all things center in Christ. He is the Firstborn of the Father. By obedience and devotion to the truth he attained that pinnacle of intelligence which ranked him as a God..."[94]

What the Bible says:
"But unto the Son he saith, Thy throne, O God, is for ever and ever..." (Hebrews 1:8)

---

92) *Journal of Discourses*, vol. 6, p. 163.
93) Hunter, *The Gospel Through the Ages*, p. 51.
94) McConkie, *Mormon Doctrine*, p. 129.

Secret 34

Mormon leaders admit that the Jesus Christ of Mormonism is NOT the Jesus Christ of Christianity:

> "...the Christ followed by the Mormons is not the Christ followed by traditional Christianity." [95]

> "In bearing testimony of Jesus Christ, President Hinckley spoke of those outside the Church who say Latter-day Saints 'do not believe in the traditional Christ.' 'No, I don't. The traditional Christ of whom they speak is not the Christ of whom I speak." [96]

> "As a Church we have critics, many of them. They say we do not believe in the traditional Christ of Christianity. There is substance to what they say." [97]

What the Bible says:

> "...Take heed lest any man deceive you: For many shall come in my name, saying, I am Christ; and shall deceive many." (Mark 13:5-6)

See also Matthew 24:23-24, Mark 13:21-22.

Secret 35

Mormons believe that Lucifer is the spirit brother of Jesus Christ:

> "The appointment of Jesus to be the Savior of the world was contested by one of the

---

95) Bernard P. Brockbank, *The Ensign*, May 1977, p. 26.
96) Gordon B. Hinckley, *LDS Church News*, week ending June 20, 1998, p. 7.
97) Gordon B. Hinckley, 172nd General Conference, April, 2002.

other sons of God. He was called Lucifer, son of the morning. Haughty, ambitious, and covetous of power and glory, this spirit—brother of Jesus desperately tried to become the Savior of mankind." [98]

"All men in pre-existence were the spirit children of God our Father, an exalted, glorified, and perfected Man... 'I was in the beginning with the Father, and am the first born,' Christ says of himself...The devil... is a spirit son of God who was born in the morning of pre-existence..." [99]

What the Bible says:

The Bible says that Satan was an archangel who fell from heaven because he wanted to be like God:

> "How art thou fallen from heaven, O Lucifer, son of the morning! how art thou cut down to the ground, which didst weaken the nations! For thou hast said in thine heart, I will ascend into heaven, I will exalt my throne above the stars of God: I will sit also upon the mount of the congregation, in the sides of the north: I will ascend above the heights of the clouds; I will be like the most High. Yet thou shalt be brought down to hell, to the sides of the pit." (Isaiah 14:12-15)

They are not brothers. Jesus Christ created Lucifer:

---

98) Hunter, *The Gospel Through the Ages*, p. 15.
99) McConkie, *Mormon Doctrine*, pp. 750, 192.

"In the beginning was the Word, and the Word was with God, and the Word was God... All things were made by him; and without him was not any thing made that was made." (John 1:1,3)

Secret 36

Mormon doctrine says Christ's blood had to be shed because Adam had no blood before the fall:

"The reason that the blood of Christ had to be shed is because Adam was without blood before the fall. The blood came into his body afterwards. Therefore, it was necessary that the blood which came by the fall should be shed in atonement." [100]

What the Bible says:

Adam had to have blood because the Bible plainly states:

"For the life of the flesh is in the blood..." (Leviticus 17:11)

THE HOLY SPIRIT

Secret 37

Mormonism teaches that the Holy Spirit is not omnipresent:

"The Holy Ghost is the third member of the Godhead. He is a Spirit, in the form of a man... The Holy Ghost is a personage

---

[100] Smith, *Answers to Gospel Questions,* vol. 3, p. 207.

of Spirit, and has a spirit body only... As a Spirit personage the Holy Ghost has size and dimensions. He does not fill the immensity of space, and cannot be everywhere present in person at the same time."[101]

What the Bible says:

"Whither shall I go from thy spirit? or whither shall I flee from thy presence? If I ascend up into heaven, thou art there: if I make my bed in hell, behold, thou art there. If I take the wings of the morning, and dwell in the uttermost parts of the sea; Even there shall thy hand lead me, and thy right hand shall hold me." (Psalm 139:7-10)

See also 1 Corinthians 3:16.

Secret 38

Mormonism teaches that the Holy Spirit is a spirit man:

"The Church of Jesus Christ of Latter-day Saints teaches that the Holy Ghost is a spirit man, a spirit son of GOD THE FATHER."[102]

What the Bible says:

"Even the Spirit of truth; whom the world cannot receive, because it seeth him not, neither knoweth him: but ye know him; for he dwelleth with you, and shall be in you." (John 14:17)

---

101) Smith, *Doctrines of Salvation*, vol. 1, p. 38.
102) Encyclopedia of Mormonism, vol. 2, p. 649.

Secret 39

Joseph Smith taught that when Gentiles become a Mormon, the Holy Ghost removes their Gentile blood and replaces it with Israelite blood:

> "The effect of the Holy Ghost upon a Gentile, is to purge out the old blood, and make him actually of the seed of Abraham. That man that has none of the blood of Abraham (naturally) must have a new creation by the Holy Ghost. In such a case, there may be more of a powerful effect upon the body, and visible to the eye, than upon an Israelite, while the Israelite at first might be far before the Gentile in pure intelligence." [103]

What the Bible says:

The Bible says nothing about this bizarre Mormon doctrine.

SALVATION

Secret 40

Mormonism teaches that obedience to the law is necessary for salvation:

> "...except ye shall keep the commandments of God ye shall all likewise perish;" [104]

> "We believe that through the Atonement of

---

103) Smith, *Teachings of The Prophet Joseph Smith*, pp. 149-150.
104) Book of Mormon, 2 Nephi 30:1.

Christ, all mankind may be saved, by obedience to the laws and ordinances of the Gospel." [105]

"...a code of laws and commandments whereby we might attain perfection and, eventually, godhood. This set of laws and ordinances is known as the gospel of Jesus Christ, and it is the only plan which will exalt mankind." [106]

"The gospel of Jesus Christ is the plan of salvation. It embraces all of the laws, principles, doctrines, rites, ordinances, acts powers, authorities, and keys necessary to save and exalt men in the highest heaven hereafter..." [107]

Eternal life, the kind of life enjoyed by eternal beings in the celestial kingdom, comes by grace plus obedience." [108]

"To enter the celestial [kingdom] and obtain exaltation, it is necessary that the whole law be kept... Do you desire to enter the celestial Kingdom and receive eternal life? Then be willing to keep all of the commandments." [109]

What the Bible says:

"Not by works of righteousness which we

---

105) Articles of Faith #3 and #4.
106) Kimball, *The Miracle of Forgiveness*, p. 6.
107) McConkie, *Mormon Doctrine*, pp. 331, 334.
108) Ibid., pp. 669-671.
109) Joseph Fielding Smith, *The Way to Perfection*, p. 206.

have done, but according to his mercy he saved us… (Titus 3:5)

See also Galatians 2:16, Ephesians 2:8-9, 2 Timothy 1:9.

Secret 41

Mormonism teaches that Temple Marriage is necessary for the highest exaltation after death:

"Marriage is not only a righteous institution, but obedience to this law [Temple marriage] is absolutely necessary in order to obtain the highest exaltation in the Kingdom of God."[110]

What the Bible says:

"Who hath saved us, and called us with an holy calling, not according to our works, but according to his own purpose and grace, which was given us in Christ Jesus before the world began," (2 Timothy 1:9)

Secret 42

Mormon doctrine teaches that sins are forgiven through good works:

"Eternal life hangs in the balance awaiting the works of men."[111]

"Repentance, baptism, and enduring in righteousness to the end comprise the course whereby sins are remitted."[112]

---

110) Hunter, *Gospel Through the Ages,* p. 119.
111) Kimball, *The Miracle of Forgiveness,* p. 208.
112) McConkie, *Mormon Doctrine,* p. 736.

> "…redemption from personal sins can only be obtained through obedience to the requirements of the gospel, and a life of good works." [113]

> "…for we know that it is by grace that we are saved, after all we can do." [114]

> "…however powerful the saving grace of Christ, it brings exaltation to no man who does not comply with the works of the gospel." [115]

> "That by keeping the commandments they might be washed and cleansed from all their sins…" [116]

> "We believe that through the Atonement of Christ, all mankind may be saved, by obedience to the laws and ordinances of the Gospel." [117]

When Joseph Smith was asked "Will everybody be damned, but Mormons?" he replied:

> "Yes, and a great portion of them, unless they repent, and work righteousness." [118]

What the Bible says:

> "Even when we were dead in sins, hath quickened us together with Christ, (by grace ye are saved;)" (Ephesians 2:5)

---

113) Talmage, *Articles of Faith,* p. 478.
114) Book of Mormon, 2 Nephi 25:23.
115) Kimball, *The Miracle of Forgiveness,* p. 207.
116) Doctrine and Covenants 76:52.
117) Article of Faith #3.
118) Smith, *Teachings of the Prophet Joseph Smith,* p. 119.

Secret 43

Mormonism says salvation by faith alone in Jesus Christ is "utter nonsense:"

"Christians speak often of the blood of Christ and its cleansing power. Much that is believed and taught on this subject, however is such utter nonsense and so palpably false that to believe it is to lose one's salvation. Many go so far, for instance, as to pretend, at least, to believe that if we confess Christ with our lips and avow that we accept him as our personal Savior, we are thereby saved. His blood, without other act than mere belief, they say, makes us clean."[119]

What the Bible says:

"But the natural man receiveth not the things of the Spirit of God: for they are foolishness unto him: neither can he know them, because they are spiritually discerned." (1 Corinthians 2:14)

Secret 44

Mormonism teaches that the doctrine of salvation by grace alone was started by Satan:

"One of the most fallacious doctrines originated by Satan and propounded by man is that man is saved alone by the grace of God; that belief in Jesus Christ alone is all that is needed for salvation…"[120]

---

119) LDS pamphlet *What the Mormons Think of Christ*, p. 32.
120) Kimball, *The Miracle of Forgiveness*, p. 206.

What the Bible says:
> "Who hath saved us, and called us with an holy calling, not according to our works, but according to his own purpose and grace, which was given us in Christ Jesus before the world began…" (2 Timothy 1:9)

> "Therefore we conclude that a man is justified by faith without the deeds of the law." (Romans 3:28)

See also Romans 6:23; 10:4, Galatians 2:21.

Secret 45

Mormonism teaches that there are two types of salvation: Unconditional:

> "Unconditional or general salvation… consists in the mere fact of being resurrected… Those who gain only this general or unconditional salvation will… therefore, be damned; their eternal progression will be cut short; they… in eternity will be ministering servants to more worthy persons… Immortality is a free gift and comes without works or righteousness of any sort; all men will come forth in the resurrection because of the atoning sacrifice of Christ… In and of itself the resurrection is a form of salvation meaning that men are thereby saved from death, hell, the devil, and endless torment…"[121]

---

121) McConkie, *Mormon Doctrine*, pp. 669, 671.

Conditional: "Conditional or individual salvation, that which comes by grace coupled with gospel obedience, consists in receiving an inheritance in the celestial kingdom of God. This kind of salvation follows faith, repentance, baptism, receipt of the Holy Ghost, and continued righteousness to the end of one's mortal probation... full salvation is obtained in and through the continuation of the family unit in eternity, and those who gain it are gods... Salvation in the celestial kingdom of God, however, is not salvation by grace alone. Rather, it is salvation by grace coupled with obedience to the laws and ordinances of the gospel... Eternal life, the kind of life enjoyed by eternal beings in the celestial kingdom, comes by grace plus obedience."[122]

What the Bible says:

The Bible never mentions different types of salvation. You are either saved or lost:

> "For the Son of man is come to seek and to save that which was lost." (Luke 19:10)

Once your sins have been cleansed by the blood of Christ, you are saved. You cannot get *more* saved:

See also Romans 3:24-25; 4:4-5; 5:1,9; 10:9-10; 10:13, Ephesians 2:5.

---

122) McConkie, *Mormon Doctrine*, pp. 669-671.

BLOOD ATONEMENT
Secret 46
Many early Mormons taught that some sins were so bad the person's own blood had to shed for their forgiveness:

Mormon President Joseph Fielding Smith taught:

"But man may commit certain grievous sins—according to his light and knowledge that will place him beyond the reach of the atoning blood of Christ. If then he would be saved he must make sacrifice of his own life to atone—so far as is in his power lies—for that sin, for the blood of Christ alone under certain circumstances will not avail…

"Joseph Smith taught that there were certain sins so grievous that man may commit, that they will place the transgressors beyond the power of the atonement of Christ. If these offenses are committed, then the blood of Christ will not cleanse them from their sins even though they repent. Therefore their only hope is to have their own blood shed to atone, as far as possible, in their behalf." [123]

Brigham Young added:

"There are sins that men commit for which they cannot receive forgiveness in this world, or in that which is to come, and if they had their eyes open to see their true condition,

---
123) Smith, *Doctrines of Salvation,* vol. 1, p. 134-135.

they would be perfectly willing to have their blood spilt upon the ground, that the smoke thereof might ascend to heaven as an offering for their sins…" [124]

"I know, when you hear my brethren telling about cutting people off from the earth, that you consider it a strong doctrine; but it is to save them, not to destroy them." [125]

"There is not a man or woman, who violates the covenants made with their God, that will not be required to pay the debt. The blood of Christ will never wipe that out, your own blood must atone for it…" [126]

"Will you love your brothers or sisters likewise, when they have committed a sin that cannot be atoned for without the shedding of their blood? Will you love that man or woman well enough to shed their blood?… I have known a great many men who have left this church for whom there is no chance whatever for exaltation, but if their blood had been spilled, it would have been better for them." [127]

Mormon apostle Jedediah Morgan Grant agreed:

"We have those amongst us that are full of all manner of abominations, those who need to

---

[124] *Journal of Discourses*, vol. 4, p. 53.
[125] Ibid., p. 53.
[126] *Journal of Discourses*, vol. 3, p. 247.
[127] Ibid., vol. 4, pp. 219-220.

have their blood shed, for water will not do, their sins are too deep a dye... And you who have committed sins that cannot be forgiven through baptism, let your blood be shed..." [128]

Bruce McConkie added:

"But under certain circumstances there are some serious sins for which the cleansing of Christ does not operate, and the law of God is that men must then have their own blood shed to atone for their sins..." [129]

What the Bible says:

"...the blood of Jesus Christ his Son cleanseth us from all sin." (1 John 1:7)

See also 1 Peter 1:18-19, Hebrews 9:11-14; 10:29, Romans 5:9, Ephesians 1:7; 2:13, Colossians 1:14, John 3:16, Revelation 1:5.

Secret 47

Because the doctrine of Blood Atonement is so embarrassing, Mormons want to convince you it never existed:

Mormon apostle Bruce McConkie wrote:

"...wicked and evilly-disposed persons have fabricated false and slanderous stories to the effect that the Church, in the early days of this dispensation, engaged in a practice of blood atonement... By taking one sentence

---

128) *Journal of Discourses*, vol. 4, pp. 49, 51.
129) McConkie, *Mormon Doctrine*, p. 92.

on one page and another from a succeeding page and even by taking a part of a sentence on one page and a part of another found several pages away—all wholly torn from context—dishonest persons have attempted to make it appear that Brigham Young and others taught things just the opposite of what they really believed and taught." [130]

THE BIBLE

Secret 48

Mormonism says the Bible is imperfect and can't be relied upon:

"We believe the Bible to be the word of God as far as it is translated correctly..." [131]

"...What shall we say then, concerning the Bible's being a sufficient guide? Can we rely upon it in its present known corrupted state, as being a faithful record of God's Word?... What few have come down to our day, have been mutilated, changed, and corrupted, in such a shameful manner that no two manuscripts agree... and all this imperfection to the uncertainty of the translation, and who, in his right mind, could, for one moment, suppose the Bible in its present form to be a perfect guide?" [132]

---

130) McConkie, *Mormon Doctrine*, p. 92.
131) Article of Faith #8.
132) Orson Pratt, *The Bible Alone, An Insufficient Guide*, pp. 44-47.

"I believe the Bible as it read when it came from the pen of the original writers. Ignorant translators, careless transcribers, or designing and corrupt priests have committed many errors."[133]

What the Bible says:

"The words of the LORD are pure words: as silver tried in a furnace of earth, purified seven times. Thou shalt keep them, O LORD, thou shalt preserve them from this generation for ever." (Psalm 12:6-7)

See also Matthew 24:35, Psalm 119:89,160, Isaiah 40:8, John 17:17, 2 Peter 1:20-21.

Secret 49

Mormon doctrine says the Word of God shall be added to:

"Wo be unto him that shall say: We have received the word of God, and we need no more of the word of God, for we have enough!"[134]

"...A Bible! A Bible! We have got a Bible, and there cannot be any more Bible... Thou fool that shall say: A Bible, we have got a Bible, and we need no more Bible... Wherefore, because that ye have a Bible ye need not suppose that it contains all my words; neither need ye suppose that I have not caused more to be written."[135]

---

133) Smith, *Teachings of the Prophet Joseph Smith*, p. 327.
134) Book of Mormon, 2 Nephi 28:29
135) Ibid., 2 Nephi 29:3, 6,10.

"One of the great heresies of modern Christendom is the unfounded assumption that the Bible contains all of the inspired teachings now extant among men."[136]

What the Bible says:
"For I testify unto every man that heareth the words of the prophecy of this book, If any man shall add unto these things, God shall add unto him the plagues that are written in this book: And if any man shall take away from the words of the book of this prophecy, God shall take away his part out of the book of life, and out of the holy city, and from the things which are written in this book." (Revelation 22:18-19)

THE BOOK OF MORMON

Secret 50

Mormonism claims the Book of Mormon is far superior to the Bible:

"The book of Mormon is more correct than the Bible…"[137]

"Almost all of the doctrines of the gospel are taught in the Book of Mormon with much greater clarity and perfection than those same

---

136) McConkie, *Mormon Doctrine*, p. 83.
137) Smith, *History of the Church,* vol. 4, p. 461.

doctrines are revealed in the Bible. Anyone who will place in parallel columns the teachings of these two great books on such subjects… will find conclusive proof of the superiority of the Book of Mormon teachings." [138]

"Joseph Smith himself declared:

"I told the brethren that the Book of Mormon was the most correct book of any on earth, and the keystone of our religion, and a man would get nearer to God by abiding by its precepts, than by any other book." [139]

What the Bible says:

"The law of the LORD is perfect, converting the soul: the testimony of the LORD is sure, making wise the simple." (Psalm 19:7)

"Sanctify them through thy truth: thy word is truth." (John 17:17)

Secret 51

A Mormon apostle admits the Book of Mormon has a familiar spirit:

"…the only way a dead people could speak 'out of the ground' or 'low out of the dust' would be by the written word, and this the people did through the book of Mormon. Truly it has a familiar spirit…" [140]

---
138) McConkie, *Mormon Doctrine*, p. 99.
139) Smith, *History of the Church*, vol. 4, p. 461.
140) LeGrand Richards, *Marvelous Work and a Wonder,* 1979 edition, pp. 67-68.

What the Bible says:

Every time the Bible mentions familiar spirits, it is referring to demonic forces. See Leviticus 20:27, 1 Samuel 28:7-8, 1 Chronicles 10:13, 2 Chronicles 33:6, Isaiah 19:3, Isaiah 29:4.

Secret 52

Mormonism teaches that all who reject the Book of Mormon will go to hell:

> "What does the Lord require of the people of the United States? He requires them to repent of all their sins and embrace the message of salvation contained in the Book of Mormon, and be baptized into this church... What will be the consequences if they do not embrace the Book of Mormon, as a divine revelation? They will be destroyed from the land and sent down to hell... There is no other alternative; they must either embrace the Book of Mormon as a divine revelation, or be cut off..."[141]

What the Bible says:

> "He that rejecteth me, and receiveth not my words, hath one that judgeth him: the word that I have spoken, the same shall judge him in the last day." (John 12:48)

---

141) Pratt, *The Seer,* p. 215.

Secret 53

Mormonism teaches that you must accept the Book of Mormon to be saved:

"The Book of Mormon claims to be a divinely inspired record... It professes to be revealed to the present generation for the salvation of all who will receive it, and for the overthrow and damnation of all nations who reject it.

"The nature of the message in the Book of Mormon is such, that if true, no one can possibly be saved and reject it; if false, no one can possibly be saved and receive it."[142]

What the Bible says:
"And it shall come to pass, that whosoever shall call on the name of the Lord shall be saved." (Acts 2:21)

MORMON CHURCH: ONLY WAY TO HEAVEN

Secret 54

The Mormon religion teaches that there is no salvation outside the Mormon church:

"There is no salvation outside the Church of Jesus Christ of Latter-day Saints."[143]

---

142) Orson Pratt, *Divine Authenticity of the Book of Mormon,* pp. 1-2.
143) McConkie, *Mormon Doctrine,* p. 670.

"...You may wander east, west, north, and south, and you cannot find it in any church or government on the earth, except the Church of Jesus Christ of Latter-day Saints." [144]

Former Mormon president Ezra Taft Benson stated:

"This is not just another Church. This is not just one of a family of Christian churches. This is THE Church and kingdom of God, THE only true Church upon the face of the earth..." [145]

"This is 'the only true and living church upon the face of the whole earth' (D. & C. 1:30) the only organization authorized by the Almighty to preach his gospel and administer the ordinances of salvation, the only Church which has power to save and exalt men in the hereafter... There is no salvation outside this one true Church, the Church of Jesus Christ." [146]

"The Church of Jesus Christ of Latter-day Saints is the sole repository of this priceless program in its fullness... In order to reach the goal of eternal life and exaltation and godhood, one must be initiated into the Kingdom by baptism, properly performed; one must receive the Holy Ghost by the laying on of authoritative hands... one must be

---

144) *Journal of Discourses*, vol. 6, p. 24.
145) Teachings of Ezra Taft Benson, pp. 164-165
146) McConkie, *Mormon Doctrine*, pp. 136-138.

endowed and sealed in the house of God... and one must live a life of righteousness, cleanliness, purity, and service." [147]

"The true gospel of Jesus Christ was restored to earth in the last days through the instrumentality of Joseph Smith. It is found only in The Church of Jesus Christ of Latter-day Saints." [148]

"This Church is the ensign on the mountain spoken of by the Old Testament prophets. It is the way, the truth, and the life." [149]

What the Bible says:

"For God so loved the world, that he gave his only begotten Son, that whosoever believeth in him should not perish, but have everlasting life." (John 3:16)

JOSEPH SMITH

Secret 55

Joseph Smith claimed that God the Father and Jesus Christ appeared to him in secret:

"...I retired to the woods... I kneeled down and began to offer up the desires of my heart to God when... I saw a pillar of light exactly

---

147) Kimball, *The Miracle of Forgiveness,* p. 6.
148) McConkie, *Mormon Doctrine,* pp. 331, 334.
149) Marion Romney (LDS First Presidency), Conference Report, April, 1961, p. 119.

over my head… When the light rested upon me I saw two Personages… standing above me in the air. One of them spake unto me, calling me by name, and said, pointing to the other. This is My Beloved Son. Hear Him!" [150]

What the Bible says:
"Then if any man shall say unto you, Lo, here is Christ, or there; believe it not. For there shall arise false Christs, and false prophets, and shall shew great signs and wonders; insomuch that, if it were possible, they shall deceive the very elect." (Matthew 24:23-24)

See also Mark 13:5, 21-22, 2 Corinthians 11:14-15.

Secret 56

Joseph Smith was arrested, thrown in jail and charged with treason:

After having declared martial law and ordered the destruction of a printing press that exposed Joseph Smith's polygamy:

"Joseph and Hiram Smith were arrested on charge of treason, and committed to await examination." [151]

What the Bible says:
"Obey them that have the rule over you, and submit yourselves…" (Hebrews 13:17)

---
150) Pearl of Great Price, Joseph Smith History, 1:14-17.
151) Edward Bonney, *Banditti of the Prairies,* 1963, pp. 20-24.

Secret 57
While he was in jail, Joseph Smith shot three men in a gun battle, killing two of them, before he was shot and killed: [152]

Although most Mormons believe Joseph Smith died as a "lamb to the slaughter," like Jesus, he went out in a blazing gunfight, killing two men before he died. Lambs do not fight for their life with their six shooters blasting.

Mormon president John Taylor said of Joseph Smith:

> "He, however, instantly arose, and with a firm, quick step, and a determined expression of countenance, approached the door, and pulling the six-shooter left by Brother Whellock from his pocket, opened the door slightly, and snapped the pistol six successive times; only three of the barrels, however, were discharged. I afterwards understood that two or three were wounded by these discharges, two of whom, I am informed died." [153]

What the Bible says:
"Thou shalt not kill." (Exodus 20:13)

Secret 58
One of Joseph Smith's wives was 14 years old:

> "Joseph deceived Emma when he proposed to 14 year old Helen Mar Kimball as a plural wife. She agreed to marry Joseph because he told her that it 'will ensure your eternal sal-

---
152) Smith, *History of The Church*, vol. 6, pp. 617-618, vol. 7, pp. 102-103.
153) Ibid., vol. 7, pp. 102-103.

vation and exaltation and that… of your father's household and all of your kindred.' She remarked, 'I willingly gave myself to purchase so glorious a reward.'" [154]

What the Bible says:

"But whoso shall offend one of these little ones which believe in me, it were better for him that a millstone were hanged about his neck, and that he were drowned in the depth of the sea." (Matthew 18:6)

Secret 59

Joseph Smith taught that people lived on the moon:

Oliver B. Huntington wrote in a Mormon magazine:

"As far back as 1837, I know that he (Joseph Smith) said the moon was inhabited by men and women the same as this earth, and that they lived to a greater age than we do—that they live generally to near the age of a 1000 years." [155]

Huntington also wrote:

"The inhabitants of the moon are more of a uniform size than the inhabitants of the earth, being about 6 feet in height. They dress very much like the Quaker style and are quite general in style or the one fashion

---

154) Emma Hale Smith, *Mormon Enigma*, pp. 146-147; Todd Compton, *In Sacred Loneliness*, p. 499); quoted at: www.mormonthink.com/lying.htm
155) *The Young Woman's Journal,* vol. 3, p. 263.

of dress. They live to be very old; coming generally, near a thousand years. This is the description of them as given by Joseph the Seer, and he could 'See' whatever he asked the Father in the name of Jesus to see."[156]

Are Mormons still defending this outrageous belief? In 1995, Mormon author Stephen W. Gibson wrote that Joseph Smith's beliefs could not be discounted simply because "…a handful of astronauts didn't see any inhabitants in the tiny area they viewed when they landed on the moon decades ago…" He insisted that "…man has no scientific or revealed knowledge of whether or not there are inhabitants on the earth's moon."[157]

Secret 60

Joseph Smith said God told him ALL creeds were an abomination:

"My object in going to inquire of the Lord was to know which of all the sects was right, that I might know which to join… I asked the Personages who stood above me in the light, which of all the sects was right… and which I should join. I was answered that I must join none of them, for they were all wrong; and the Personage who addressed me said that all their creeds were an abomination in his sight; that those professors were all cor-

---

156) *The History of Oliver B. Huntington,* p. 10, typed copy, Marriott Library, University of Utah.
157) Stephen W. Gibson, *One-Minute Answers to Anti-Mormon Questions,* p. 80.

rupt…He again forbade me to join with any of them…"[158]

What the Bible says:

"That thou art Peter, and upon this rock I will build my church; and the gates of hell shall not prevail against it." (Matthew 16:18)

See also 1 Corinthians 3:11, Ephesians 2:20; 3:21, Acts 2:47, Matthew 28:18-20.

Secret 61

Joseph Smith had some very strange teaching about angels:

"How, it may be asked, was this known to be a bad angel? By the color of his hair; that is one of the signs that he can be known by…"[159]

Secret 62

Brigham Young claimed that everyone who denies that Joseph Smith is a Prophet is of anti-Christ:

"Every spirit that confesses that Joseph Smith is a Prophet, that he lived and died a Prophet and that the Book of Mormon is true, is of God, and every spirit that does not is of anti-Christ."[160]

What the Bible says:

This is a twisting of 1 John 4:2-3, removing Jesus Christ and replacing Him with Joseph Smith:

---

158) Pearl of Great Price, Joseph Smith History, 1:14-20.
159) Smith, *History of the Church,* vol. 4, p. 581.
160) Ibid., vol. 7, p. 287.

"Every spirit that confesseth that Jesus Christ is come in the flesh is of God: And every spirit that confesseth not that Jesus Christ is come in the flesh is not of God: and this is that spirit of antichrist…" (1 John 4:2-3)

Secret 63

Joseph Smith claimed he was greater than Jesus Christ:

"…I have more to boast of than any man had. I am the only man that has ever been able to keep a whole church together since the days of Adam. A large majority of the whole have stood by me. Neither Paul, John, Peter, nor Jesus ever did it. I boast that no man ever did such a work as I. The followers of Jesus ran away from Him; but the Latter-day Saints never ran away from me yet."[161]

What the Bible says:

"Pride goeth before destruction, and an haughty spirit before a fall." (Proverbs 16:18)

Secret 64

Joseph Smith claimed he knew more than all the world put together:

"Now, I ask who hear me, why the learned men who are preaching salvation say that God created the heavens and the earth out of nothing? The reason is, that they are unlearned in the things of God. …But I am

---

161) Smith, *History of the Church,* vol. 6, pp. 408-409.

learned, and know more than all the world put together." [162]

What the Bible says:

"For I say, through the grace given unto me, to every man that is among you, not to think of himself more highly than he ought to think; but to think soberly, according as God hath dealt to every man the measure of faith." (Romans 12:3)

Secret 65

Joseph Smith claimed that certain sins could not be forgiven:

"A murderer, for instance, one that sheds innocent blood, cannot have forgiveness." [163]

What the Bible says:

"In whom we have redemption through his blood, even the forgiveness of sins:" (Colossians 1:14)

Secret 66

Without Joseph Smith, there would be no salvation:

"If it had not been for Joseph Smith and the restoration, there would be no salvation." [164]

Joseph Fielding Smith said:

"There is no salvation without accepting Joseph Smith as a prophet of God... If

---

162) *Journal of Discourses*, vol. 6, p. 5.
163) Smith, *Teachings of the Prophet Joseph Smith*, p. 339.
164) McConkie, *Mormon Doctrine*, p. 670.

> Joseph Smith was verily a prophet, and if he told the truth...no man can reject that testimony without incurring the most dreadful consequences, for he cannot enter the kingdom of God." [165]

> "It is because the Lord called Joseph Smith that salvation is again available to mortal men." [166]

> "...no man or woman in this dispensation will ever enter into the celestial kingdom of God without the consent of Joseph Smith... every man and woman must have the certificate of Joseph Smith, junior, as a passport to their entrance into the mansion where God and Christ are—I with you and you with me. I cannot go there without his consent." [167]

Former Mormon apostle George Q. Cannon declared:

> "If we get our salvation, we shall have to pass by him [Joseph Smith]; if we enter our glory, it will be through the authority he has received. We cannot get around him [Joseph Smith]." [168]

> "Every spirit that confesses that Joseph Smith is a Prophet, that he lived and died a Prophet and that the Book of Mormon is true, is of

---

165) Smith, *Doctrines of Salvation,* vol. 1, pp. 188, 190.
166) McConkie, *Mormon Doctrine*, p. 396.
167) *Journal of Discourses*, vol. 7, p. 289.
168) Melchizedek Priesthood Study Guide, p. 142, 1988.

God, and every spirit that does not is of anti-Christ."[169]

What the Bible says:
"Jesus saith unto him, I am the way, the truth, and the life: no man cometh unto the Father, but by me." (John 14:6)

See also Matthew 1:21, Luke 2:11, John 1:12; 3:17, 36; 10:1,9, Acts 4:12; 16:30-31, 1 Timothy 2:5, Philippians 2:10-11, Hebrews 7:25, 1 John 3:23; 5:12, Jude 25.

Secret 67

Joseph Smith was undeniably involved in treasure-seeking and magic:

"As historian Richard L. Bushman has written: 'There had always been evidence of it ('money-digging in the Smith family') in the hostile affidavits from the Smith's neighbors, evidence which Mormons dismissed as hopelessly biased. But when I got into the sources, I found evidence from friendly contemporaries as well, Martin Harris, Joseph Knight, Oliver Cowdery, and Lucy Mack Smith. All of these witnesses persuaded me treasure-seeking and vernacular magic were part of the Smith family tradition, and that the hostile witnesses, including the 1826 trial record, had to be taken seriously.'"[170]

---
169) Smith, *History of the Church,* vol. 7, p. 287.
170) D. Michael Quinn, *Early Mormonism and the Magic World View,* p. 59.

Brigham Young University historian Marvin S. Hill also admits:

> "Now, most historians, Mormon or not, who work with the sources, accept as fact Joseph Smith's career as village magician."[171]

What the Bible says:
> "Therefore hearken not ye to your prophets, nor to your diviners, nor to your dreamers, nor to your enchanters, nor to your sorcerers, which speak unto you..." (Jeremiah 27:9)

Secret 68

Joseph Smith was involved in occultic practices:

Joseph Smith was known to use seer stones and divining rods. He even had a magic Jupiter talisman on him when he died.[172] He used seer stones to look for buried treasure in the earth. He was arrested and brought before a Justice of the Peace on March 20, 1826 and formally charged and found guilty of "glass looking."

What the Bible says:
> "There shall not be found among you any one that... useth divination, or an observer of times, or an enchanter, or a witch, Or a charmer, or a consulter with familiar spirits, or a wizard, or a necromancer. For all that do these things are an abomination unto the LORD: and because of these abominations

---
171) D. Michael Quinn, *Early Mormonism and the Magic World View*, p. 59.
172) David Martin, *Mormon Miscellaneous*, 1975, vol. 1, pp. 14-15.

the LORD thy God doth drive them out from before thee." (Deuteronomy 18:10-12)

Secret 69
One man's testimony about Joseph Smith:

"I first became acquainted with Joseph Smith, Jr. in November, 1825. He was at that time in the employ of a set of men who were called 'money diggers;' and his occupation was that of seeing, or pretending to see by means of a stone placed in his hat, and his hat closed over his face. In this way he pretended to discover minerals and hidden treasure... young Smith... asked my consent to his marrying my daughter Emma. This I refused... he was a stranger, and followed a business that I could not approve... while I was absent from home [he] carried off my daughter... they were married...

In a short time they returned... Smith stated to me that he had given up what he called 'glass looking...' He also made arrangements with my son... to go up to Palmyra... after this, I was informed they had brought a wonderful book of plates down with them...

The manner in which he pretended to read and interpret, was the same as when he looked for the 'money diggers' with the stone in his

Secrets Mormons Don't Want You To Know 73

hat, and his hat over his face, while the book of plates was at the same time hid in the woods!" [173]

What the Bible says:
 "...be sure your sin will find you out."
 (Numbers 32:23)

Secret 70

Mormon writings were changed to cover up Joseph Smith's occultic practices:

The 1833 printing of the *Book of Commandments,* (now called the Doctrine and Covenants) openly spoke about Joseph Smith's use of his divining rod:

"Now this is not all, for you have another gift, which is the gift of *working with the rod:* behold it has told you things: behold there is no other power save God, that can cause *this rod of nature,* to work in your hands..." [174]

However, the 1835 edition of Doctrine and Covenants changes the phrases "the gift of working with the rod" and "this rod of nature" to the "gift of Aaron." [175]

"Now this is not all thy gift, for you have another gift, which is the *gift of Aaron;* behold, it has told you many things; Behold, there is no other power, save the power of God, that can cause this *gift of Aaron* to be with you." [176]

---

173) Affidavit of Isaac Hale, in the New York Baptist Register, June 13, 1834.
174) Book of Commandments 7:3, 1833 printing.
175) Doctrine and covenants 8:6-7.
176) Ibid.

What the Bible says:
> "…there is nothing covered, that shall not be revealed; and hid, that shall not be known." (Matthew 10:26)

Secret 71
Joseph Smith used a magic hat to translate the Book of Mormon:

David Whitmer was an early Mormon who claimed he was present when Joseph Smith translated the golden plates. Here is his description of what occurred:

> "I will now give you a description of the manner in which the Book of Mormon was translated. Joseph Smith would put the seer stone into a hat, and put his face into the hat, drawing it closely around his face to exclude the light; and in the darkness the spiritual light would shine. A piece of something resembling parchment would appear, and on that appeared the writing. One character at a time would appear, and under it was the interpretation in English. Brother Joseph would read off the English to Oliver Cowdery, who was his principal scribe, and when it was written down and repeated to Brother Joseph to see if it was correct, then it would disappear, and another character with the interpretation would appear. Thus the Book of Mormon was translated by the gift and power of God, and not by any power of man."[177]

---
177) David Whitmer, *An Address To All Believers In Christ,* p. 12.

Emma Hale Smith, Joseph Smith's wife, was his first scribe. She wrote the following to their son Joseph Smith III:

> "In writing for your father I frequently wrote day after day, often sitting at the table close to him, he sitting *with his face buried in his hat, with the stone in it,* and dictating hour after hour with nothing between us."[178]

Isaac Hale, the father of Emma Hale Smith, said of Joseph Smith in an 1834 affidavit:

> "The manner in which he pretended to read and interpret, was the same as when he looked for the money-diggers, with a stone in his hat, and his hat over his face, while the Book of Plates were at the same time hid in the woods."[179]

Michael Morse, Emma Smith's brother-in-law, gave another first-hand account of Smith's translation technique:

> "When Joseph was translating the Book of Mormon [I] had occasion more than once to go into his immediate presence, and saw him engaged at his work of translation. The mode of procedure consisted in Joseph's placing the Seer Stone in the crown of a hat, then putting his face into the hat, so as to entirely cover his face, resting his elbows upon his

---

178) Emma Smith Letter, The Saints' Herald, May 19, 1888, p. 310.
179) Affidavit of Isaac Hale dated March 20, 1834, cited in Rodger I. Anderson, *Joseph Smith's New York Reputation Reexamined,* (Salt Lake City: Signature Books, 1990), pp. 126-128.

knees, and then dictating word after word, while the scribes—Emma, John Whitmer, O. Cowdery, or some other wrote it down."[180]

What the Bible says:
"And her prophets have daubed them with untempered morter, seeing vanity, and divining lies unto them, saying, Thus saith the Lord GOD, when the LORD hath not spoken." (Ezekiel 22:28)

Secret 72
Joseph Smith claimed to author the Book of Mormon, but later Mormons changed that:

The 1830 edition of the Book of Mormon says, "By Joseph Smith, Junior, author and proprietor." But the 1981 edition changes it to, "Translated by Joseph Smith, Jun."

Secret 73
Joseph Smith fibbed about translating the Book of Abraham:

In 1835, Joseph Smith purchased some papyri from a traveler in Kirtland, Ohio. Later he announced they were the actual writings of Abraham.

> "... I commenced the translation of some of the characters or hieroglyphics, and much to our joy found that one of the rolls contained the writings of Abraham, another the writings of Joseph of Egypt..."[181]

---

180) W.W. Blair interview with Michael Morse, Saints' Herald, vol. 26, no. 12 (June 15, 1879), pp. 190-91.
181) Smith, *History of the Church,* vol. 2, p. 236.

Josiah Quincy, who saw the papyri, gives this account:

> "The prophet referred to his miraculous gift of understanding all languages… 'And now come with me,' said the prophet, 'and I will show you the curiosities…' Some parchments inscribed with hieroglyphics were then offered… 'That is the handwriting of Abraham, the Father of the Faithful,' said the prophet. 'This is the autograph of Moses, and these lines were written by his brother Aaron. Here we have the earliest account of Creation, from which Moses composed the First Book of Genesis…'" [182]

But after many years of believing that the original papyri had been destroyed in a fire, the Deseret News announced on November 17, 1967 that they had been found and returned to the Mormon church.

After examination, it turned out that these supposed writings of Abraham were part of the Egyptian "Book of Breathings," a funeral work addressed to the deceased by the chief priest conducting the funeral service." [183]

James H. Breasted, Ph. D., of the Haskell Oriental Museum, University of Chicago, said:

> "…these three facsimiles of Egyptian documents in the 'Pearl of Great Price' depict the most common objects in the mortuary

---
182) William Mulder, A. Russell Mortensen, *Among the Mormons*, pp. 136-137.
183) The Book of the Dead, Facsimiles of the Papyri of Hunefer, Anhai, Kerasher and Netchemet, London, 1899, p. 33.

religion of Egypt. Joseph Smith's interpretations of them as part of a unique revelation through Abraham, therefore, very clearly demonstrates that he was totally unacquainted with the significance these documents and absolutely ignorant of the simplest facts of Egyptian writing and civilization." [184]

In spite of the overwhelming evidence, the President of the Mormon church says their religion still accepts Book of Abraham as scripture:

"The First Presidency of the Church of Jesus Christ of Latter-day Saints accepts the 'Book of Abraham' as 'scripture given to us through the prophet,' President N. Eldon Tanner said Sunday night." [185]

What the Bible says:
"The ancient and honourable, he is the head; and the prophet that teacheth lies, he is the tail. For the leaders of this people cause them to err; and they that are led of them are destroyed." (Isaiah 9:15-16)

Secret 74

Joseph Smith claimed that God did NOT form the earth out of nothing:

"Now, I ask who hear me, why the learned men who are preaching salvation say that

---

184) Joseph Smith Jr., as a Translator, pp. 26-27.
185) Salt Lake Tribune, May 4, 1970.

God created the heavens and the earth out of nothing? The reason is, that they are unlearned in the things of God. But I am learned, and know more than all the world put together."[186]

What the Bible says:
"In the beginning God created the heaven and the earth." (Genesis 1:1)

Secret 75

Mormonism says John the Baptist personally appeared to Joseph Smith:

"John the Baptist appeared to Joseph Smith and conferred the Aaronic Priesthood upon him, and by the authority of the Priesthood he was baptized."[187]

JOSEPH SMITH'S FALSE PROPHECIES

Secret 76

Joseph Smith made many prophecies that failed to come to pass:

1) In 1835, he prophesied that Jesus Christ would return to earth within 56 years.[188] Christ didn't return by 1891.

---

186) *Journal of Discourses*, vol. 6, p. 5.
187) Weber Stake Ward Teacher's Lesson for January, 1922.
188) Smith, *History of the Church*, vol. 2, p. 182.

2) Joseph Smith prophesied that Jesus Christ would return to a city called New Jerusalem, in the state of Missouri:

> "A revelation of Jesus Christ unto his servant Joseph Smith, Jun. ... Yea, the word of the Lord concerning his church, established in the last days for the restoration of his people, as he has spoken by the mouth of his prophets, and for the gathering of his saints to stand upon Mount Zion, which shall be the city of New Jerusalem. Which city shall be built, beginning at the temple lot, which is appointed by the finger of the Lord, in the western boundaries of the State of Missouri..." [189]

3) Smith prophesied that this temple would be built in his generation:

> "Verily this is the word of the Lord, that the city New Jerusalem shall be built by the gathering of the saints, beginning at this place, even the place of the temple, which temple shall be reared in this generation. For verily this generation shall not all pass away until an house shall be built unto the Lord, and a cloud shall rest upon it, which cloud shall be even the glory of the Lord, which shall fill the house." [190]

It has been over 150 years and there is still no temple.

---

189) Doctrine and Covenants 84:1-3.
190) Ibid. 84:2-5,31.

4) Joseph Smith prophesied in 1832 that war would be poured out on all nations:

> "Verily, thus saith the Lord concerning the wars that will shortly come to pass, beginning at the rebellion of South Carolina... And the time will come when war will be poured out upon all nations, beginning at this place. For behold, the Southern States shall be divided against the Northern States, and the Southern States will call on other nations, even the nation of Great Britain, as it is called, and they shall also call upon other nations, in order to defend themselves against other nations; and then war shall be poured out upon all nations." [191]

The first part of verse 3 could apply to the Civil War, but the remaining portion failed entirely.

5) In 1832, Smith made this terrifying prophecy:

> "For not many days hence and the earth shall tremble and reel to and fro as a drunken man; and the sun shall hide his face, and shall refuse to give light; and the moon shall be bathed in blood; and the stars shall become exceedingly angry, and shall cast themselves down as a fig that falleth from off a fig-tree." [192]

6) Smith prophesied that he would possess his house in Nauvoo "forever and ever," and his seed would live

---

191) Doctrine and Covenants 87:1-3.
192) Ibid. 88:87.

there "from generation to generation." But the house was destroyed after his death and his descendants moved to Independence, Missouri.

7) Smith prophesied when Jesus Christ would return:

> "I prophesy in the name of the Lord God, and let it be written—the Son of Man will not come in the clouds of heaven till I am eighty-five years old." [193]

Smith died at the age of 39. Another false prophecy.

8) In May 1843, Joseph Smith prophesied that United States government would be utterly wasted:

> "...and I prophesy in the name of the Lord God of Israel, unless the United States redress the wrongs committed upon the Saints in the state of Missouri and punish the crimes committed by her officers that in a few years the government will be utterly overthrown and wasted, and there will not be so much as a potsherd left..." [194]

There is no evidence of the United States "redressing the wrongs committed upon the Saints." Yet the government was not "utterly overthrown or wasted."

9) On December 16, 1843, Joseph Smith spoke about a petition he had filed with Congress for protection of the Latter-day Saints:

---

193) Smith, *Teachings of the Prophet Joseph Smith,* p. 286.
194) *Documentary History of the Church,* vol. 5, p. 394.

> "While discussing the petition with Congress, I prophesied by virtue of the Holy Priesthood vested in me, and in the name of the Lord Jesus Christ, that, if Congress will not hear our petition and grant us protection, they shall be broken up as a government, and God shall damn them and there shall nothing be left of them not even a grease spot." [195]

Congress did not grant the petition and the government was obviously not broken up.

10) Joseph Smith prophesied that he would be victorious over his enemies:

> "I therefore, in behalf of the Municipal Court of Nauvoo, warn the lawless, not to be precipitate in any interference in our affairs, for as sure as there is a God in heaven, WE SHALL RIDE TRIUMPHANT OVER ALL OPPRESSION. Joseph Smith, Mayor" [196]

Eight days after making this prophecy, Joseph Smith was shot dead. Within two years, the Mormons were driven out of Illinois. Another false prophecy.

11) In September 1832, Joseph Smith prophesied that the cities of New York, Albany and Boston would be destroyed if they rejected the Mormon gospel:

> "Nevertheless, let the bishop go unto the city of New York, also to the city of Albany,

---

195) Millennial Star, vol. 22, p. 455.
196) Recorded in the *Nauvoo Neighbor,* June 19, 1844.

and also to the city of Boston, and warn the people of those cities with the sound of the gospel, with a loud voice, of the desolation and utter abolishment which await them if they do reject these things. For if they do reject these things the hour of their judgment is nigh, and their house shall be left unto them desolate." [197]

12) In 1837 Joseph Smith made the following prophecy about Apostle Thomas B. Marsh:

"Verily thus saith the Lord unto you my servant Thomas: thou shalt be exalted… and thou shalt bear record of my name, not only unto the Gentiles, but also unto the Jews; and thou shalt send forth my word unto the ends of the earth… I, the Lord, have a great work for thee to do, in publishing my name among the children of men… for thou art chosen, and thy path lieth among the mountains, and among many nations… the Lord thy God shall lead thee by the hand… I know thy heart…" [198]

Less than two years later, Thomas Marsh was excommunicated.

13) In Mormon scripture, Joseph Smith said Jesus gave him a revelation that the United Order would exist until He returned:

---

197) Doctrine and Covenants 84:114-115.
198) Ibid. 112:1-11.

> "I give unto you counsel, and a commandment, concerning all the properties which belong to the order which I commanded to be organized and established, to be a united order, and an everlasting order for the benefit of my church, and for the salvation of men until I come."[199]

Jesus hasn't returned, but the United Order disbanded decades ago.

14) Joseph Smith admitted that some of his revelations were "of the devil." When Mormons needed money to print the Book of Mormon, it was suggested that the copyright should be sold to raise the needed money. Joseph Smith was persuaded to:

> "inquire of the Lord about it. Joseph looked into the hat in which he placed the stone, and received a revelation that some of the brethren should go to Toronto, Canada, and that they would sell the copy-right of the Book of Mormon."

Despite Joseph Smith's assurance of success, the plan failed. Joseph Smith said he asked the Lord about it, and the following revelation came to him through the stone:

> "Some revelations are of God: some revelations are of man: and some revelations are of the devil." So we see that the revelation to go to Toronto and sell the copyright was

---
199) Doctrine and Covenants 104:1.

not of God, but was of the devil or of the heart of man."[200]

15) On April 17, 1838 Joseph Smith prophesied that David W. Patten would go on a mission trip with him the following spring.[201] But David W. Patten died six months later, on October 25, 1838.[202]

16) On January 4, 1833, Joseph Smith prophesied:

> "…not many years shall pass away before the United States shall present such a scene of bloodshed as has not a parallel in the history of our nation; pestilence, hail, famine, and earthquake will sweep the wicked of this generation from off the face of the land…"[203]

At the same time Smith declared:

> "…'the hour of His judgment is come.' Repent ye, repent ye, and embrace the everlasting covenant and flee to Zion, before the overflowing scourge overtake you…"[204]

It's been over 175 years, and it never happened.

17) In 1856 Brigham Young declared:

> "…twenty-six years will not pass away before the Elders of this Church will be as much thought of as the kings on their thrones."[205]

---

200) Whitmer, *An Address To All Believers In Christ,* 1887, pp. 30-31.
201) Doctrine and Covenants 114:1-2.
202) Smith, *History of the Church*, vol. 3, p. 171
203) Ibid., vol. 1, pp. 315-316.
204) Ibid.
205) *Journal of Discourses* vol. 4, pp. 40-41.

That never did happen either. Another in a long line of false prophecies.

What the Bible says:

> "When a prophet speaketh in the name of the LORD, if the thing follow not, nor come to pass, that is the thing which the LORD hath not spoken, but the prophet hath spoken it presumptuously: thou shalt not be afraid of him." (Deuteronomy 18:22)

> "How long shall this be in the heart of the prophets that prophesy lies? yea, they are prophets of the deceit of their own heart;" (Jeremiah 23:26)

BLACK PEOPLE

Secret 77

Mormon apostle Bruce McConkie said as recently as 1979 that the Negro race has been cursed with black skin:

> "...Cain, Ham, and the whole negro race have been cursed with a black skin, the mark of Cain, so they can be identified as a caste apart, a people with whom the other descendants of Adam should not intermarry."[206]

The Book of Mormon declares...

> "...the Lord God did cause a skin of blackness to come upon them. And thus saith

---

206) McConkie, *Mormon Doctrine,* 1966 edition, 1979 printing, p. 114.

> the Lord God: I will cause that they shall be loathsome..."[207]

Loathsome means "disgusting," "revolting," "repulsive." Not a very nice way to describe black people.

> "And the skins of the Lamanites were dark, according to the mark which was set upon their fathers, which was a curse upon them because of their transgression..."[208]

> "...the Lord put a mark upon him [Cain], which is the flat nose and black skin."[209]

Secret 78

The Book of Mormon says that anyone who mixes their seed with a black person shall also be cursed:

> "And cursed shall be the seed of him that amixeth with their seed; for they shall be cursed even with the same cursing. And the Lord spake it, and it was done."[210]

Secret 79

Mormonism teaches that Cain was the father of an "inferior race:"

> "Not only was Cain called upon to suffer, but because of his wickedness he became the father of an inferior race..."[211]

---

207) Book of Mormon, 2 Nephi 5:21-22
208) Book of Mormon, Alma 3:6
209) *Journal of Discourses,* vol. 7, p. 290.
210) Book of Mormon, 2 Nephi 5:23.
211) Joseph Fielding Smith, *The Way to Perfection*, pp. 101-102.

"You see some classes of the human family that are black, uncouth, uncomely, disagreeable and low in their habits, wild, and seemingly deprived of nearly all the blessings of the intelligence that is generally bestowed upon mankind. ...That curse will remain upon them, and they never can hold the Priesthood or share in it until all the other descendants of Adam have received the promises and enjoyed the blessings of the Priesthood and the keys thereof." [212]

Secret 80

According to Mormon doctrine, those who were less valiant in "pre-existence" are born on earth with black skin as a curse:

"Those who were less valiant in pre—existence and who thereby had certain spiritual restrictions imposed upon them during mortality are known to us as the negroes. Such spirits are sent to earth through the lineage of Cain, the mark put upon him for his rebellion against God and his murder of Abel being a black skin." [213]

Secret 81

Mormonism reveals how long black people will be cursed:

"When all the other children of Adam have had the privilege of receiving the Priesthood, and of coming into the kingdom of God, and

---

212) *Journal of Discourses*, vol. 7. pp. 290-291.
213) McConkie, *Mormon Doctrine*, 1958 edition, p. 527.

of being redeemed from the four quarters of the earth, and have received their resurrection from the dead, then it will be time enough to remove the curse from Cain and his posterity."[214]

Secret 82

Mormon doctrine teaches that Cain was once an associate of Lucifer:

"Though he was a rebel and an associate of Lucifer in pre-existence, and though he was a liar from the beginning whose name was Perdition, Cain managed to attain the privilege of mortal birth..."[215]

Secret 83

Joseph Fielding Smith, 10th President and Mormon Prophet, said of black people:

"...their black covering emblematical of eternal darkness."[216]

Secret 84

George Albert Smith, the 8th President of the Mormon church, declared that black people are not entitled to the full blessings of the Gospel:

"From the days of the prophet Joseph even until now, it has been the doctrine of the Church, never questioned by any of the

---

[214] *Journal of Discourses*, vol. 2, pp. 142-143.
[215] McConkie, *Mormon Doctrine*, 1958 edition, p. 109.
[216] Smith, *The Way to Perfection*, pp. 102.

Secrets Mormons Don't Want You To Know

Church leaders, that the Negroes are not entitled to the full blessings of the Gospel."[217]

Secret 85
Brigham Young declared that a white man who had sex with a black woman should be killed:

"Shall I tell you the law of God in regard to the African race? If the white man who belongs to the chosen seed mixes his blood with the seed of Cain, the penalty, under the law of God, is death on the spot. This will always be so."[218]

What the Bible says:

"…if thou kill, thou art become a transgressor of the law." (James 2:11)

Secret 86
Brigham Young taught that allowing whites to marry blacks would cause God to curse and destroy the Mormon religion:

"The moment we consent to mingle with the seed of Cain the church must go to destruction—we should receive the curse which has been placed upon the seed of Cain…"[219]

Secret 87
Until recently, blacks were refused the Mormon priesthood:

In 1954, Mormon President David O. McKay said:

"We believe that we have scriptural prec-

---
217) John J. Stewart, *Mormonism and the Negro*, 1960, pp. 46-47.
218) *Journal of Discourses*, vol. 10, p. 110.
219) Brigham Young Address, Ms d 1234, Box 48, folder 3.

edent for withholding the priesthood from the Negro."[220]

"Negroes in this life are denied the priesthood; under no circumstances can they hold this delegation of authority from the Almighty... The gospel message of salvation is not carried affirmatively to them... The negroes are not equal with other races where the receipt of certain spiritual blessings are concerned, particularly the priesthood and the temple blessings that flow therefrom, but this inequality is not of man's origin. It is the Lord's doing...[221]

What the Bible says:

"...God is no respecter of persons:" (Acts 10:34)

Secret 88

Mormon leaders refused to abandon their racist doctrine for as long as they could:

In 1967, high-ranking Mormon N. Eldon Tanner said:

"The church has no intention of changing its doctrine on the Negro. Throughout the history of the original Christian church, the negro never held the priesthood. There's really nothing we can do to change this. It's the law of God."[222]

---

220) Roger O. Porter, from article "Educator Cites McKay Statement of No Negro Bias in LDS Tenets" Salt Lake Tribune, January 15, 1970.
221) McConkie, *Mormon Doctrine*, p. 527.
222) N. Eldon Tanner, *Seattle Magazine*, Dec. 1967, p. 60.

What the Bible says:

The "law of God" is the Bible, and the Bible does not say this.

Secret 89

Blacks were not allowed into the Mormon priesthood until 1978:

Throughout the civil rights era in the 1960's, blacks were barred from the Mormon priesthood. But when athletes began boycotting Brigham Young University, lawsuits were threatened and public condemnation grew, the "revelation" finally came:

> "...we have pleaded long and earnestly in behalf of these, our faithful brethren, spending many hours in the Upper Room of the Temple supplicating the Lord for divine guidance. He has heard our prayers, and by revelation has confirmed that the long-promised day has come when every faithful, worthy man in the Church may receive the holy priesthood... Accordingly, all worthy male members of the Church may be ordained to the priesthood without regard for race or color..." [223]

Secret 90

Mormon leaders claim the real racist was God:

Several Mormon leaders claim they wanted to end the ban on racism but God would not let them:

---

223) Official Declaration–2. Salt Lake City, Utah, September 30, 1978.

"In 1954, then President David O. McKay and the Apostles of the Mormon Church studied the matter. President McKay... prayed about it, but according to his own accounts, the Lord told him the time had not yet come... In 1973, President Harold B. Lee fasted for three days and nights while praying about the issue, but received the same answer: the time had not yet come.

"Finally, in 1978, while gathered with the Quorum of the Twelve Apostles, President Spencer W. Kimball announced that he had received a revelation ending the ban."[224]

What the Bible says:

When Adam fell into sin, he blamed his sin on Eve. Eve blamed her sin on the devil. As a result, both were cast out of the garden of Eden. How much worse is it when men blame their racist doctrines on God?

Secret 91

Today, the Book of Mormon still equates black skin with rebellion against God:

"And he had caused the cursing to come upon them, yea, even a sore cursing, because of their iniquity. For behold, they had hardened their hearts against him, that they had become like unto a flint; wherefore, as they were white, and exceedingly fair and delightsome, that they might

---

224) www.meetmormonmissionaries.org/88/african_american

not be enticing unto my people the Lord God did cause a skin of blackness to come upon them." [225]

Although Bruce McConkie's book *Mormon Doctrine* received many changes concerning the doctrine of black people, the 1986 printing still states:

"The race and nation in which men are born in this world is a direct result of their pre-existent life." [226]

GOOD WORKS REDEEM THE DEAD

Secret 92

Mormonism teaches that our good works redeem the dead:

"…the greatest responsibility in this world that God has laid upon us, is to seek after our dead… It matters not what else we have been called to do… none are exempt from this great obligation… Place, distinction, or long service in the cause of Zion in the mission field, the stakes of Zion, or elsewhere will not entitle one to disregard the salvation of one's dead." [227]

"But the greatest and grandest duty of all is to labor for the dead. We may and should do all

---

225) Book of Mormon 2 Nephi 5:21.
226) McConkie, *Mormon Doctrine,* 1986 printing, p. 616.
227) Joseph Fielding Smith, Message from the First Presidency: Salvation Universal, Ensign, Feb 1971, 2.

these other things, for which reward will be given, but if we neglect the weightier privilege and commandment, notwithstanding all other good works, we shall find ourselves under severe condemnation:" [228]

"…the greatest commandment given us, and made obligatory, is the temple work in our own behalf and in behalf of our dead… The Lord expects of us all that we do what we can for ourselves and for our dead." [229]

"…we are the only people that know how to save our progenitors, how to save ourselves, and how to save our posterity…we in fact are the saviors of the world…" [230]

What the Bible says:

"When a wicked man dieth, his expectation shall perish: and the hope of unjust men perisheth." (Proverbs 11:7)

BAPTISM

Secret 93

Mormon doctrine says remission of sins comes through baptism:

'We believe… Baptism by immersion for the remission of sins…" [231]

---

228) Joseph Fielding Smith, Message from the First Presidency: Salvation Universal. Ensign, Feb 1971, 2.
229) Smith, *Doctrines of Salvation,* vol. 2, pp. 146-149.
230) *Journal of Discourses*, vol. 6, p. 163.
231) Article of Faith #4.

"Baptism... is for the remission of sins."[232]

"Initially and primarily, accountable and worthy persons gain forgiveness of their sins when a valid and authoritative baptism is performed for them. The very ordinance of baptism is ordained, among other reasons, so that man may gain a remission of their sins through it."[233]

What the Bible says:

"For this is my blood of the new testament, which is shed for many for the remission of sins." (Matthew 26:28)

Secret 94

Mormon doctrine declares that people are born again through baptism:

"The first birth takes place when spirits pass from their pre-existent first estate into mortality... The second birth begins when men are baptized in water by a legal administrator... No one can be born again without baptism..."[234]

"Baptism, a Second Birth. If one cannot see or enter into the kingdom of God without being born again, it is very important that we should fully understand what the Savior had in mind. Since he indicated that this second birth should be 'of water and of the spirit,' it

---

232) McConkie, *Mormon Doctrine*, p. 70.
233) Ibid., p. 295.
234) Ibid., p. 101.

is obvious that he had in mind the matter of being baptized in water..."[235]

"The Book of Mormon points out definitely that baptism is an ordinance of initiation, rebirth and regeneration..."[236]

"Baptism, however, is the Gospel ordinance of rebirth..."[237]

What the Bible says:
"Being born again, not of corruptible seed, but of incorruptible, by the word of God, which liveth and abideth for ever." (1 Peter 1:23)

See also John 1:12-13, John 3:3-8.

Secret 95

Mormonism teaches that whenever you sin, your past sins return:

"...but unto that soul who sinneth shall the former sins return, saith the Lord your God."[238]

"Those who feel that they can sin and be forgiven and then return to sin and be forgiven again and again must straighten out their thinking. Each previously forgiven sin is added to the new one and the whole gets to be a heavy load."[239]

---

235) LeGrand Richards, *A Marvelous Work and A Wonder*, p. 107.
236) Hunter, *The Gospel Through the Ages*, p. 196.
237) Ibid., p. 215.
238) Doctrine and Covenants 82:7.
239) Kimball, *The Miracle of Forgiveness,* p. 170.

What the Bible says:
> "As far as the east is from the west, so far hath he removed our transgressions from us." (Psalm 103:12)

See also Isaiah 1:18; 43:25, Hebrews 8:12, Revelation 1:5.

Secret 96

Mormonism teaches that all children should be baptized at the age of eight for remission of sins:

> "And their children shall be baptized for remission of their sins when eight years old, and receive the laying on of hands."[240]

> "Thus the Lord himself fixed the age of accountability at eight years, at which age children who have been taught by their parents as commanded are to be baptized."[241]

What the Bible says:
> "…they came unto a certain water: and the eunuch said, See, here is water; what doth hinder me to be baptized? And Philip said, If thou believest with all thine heart, thou mayest." (Acts 8:36-38)

Secret 97

Mormon doctrine says dead people can still enter the kingdom of God if someone is baptized for them:

Sixth Mormon president Joseph Fielding Smith (not

---
240) Doctrine and Covenants 68:27.
241) Richards, *A Marvelous Work and A Wonder,* p. 99.

to be confused with the tenth Mormon President, Joseph Fielding Smith) said:

> "But greater than all this, so far as our individual responsibilities are concerned, the greatest is to become saviors, in our lesser degree which is assigned us, for the dead who have died without a knowledge of the Gospel."[242]

Tenth Mormon president Joseph Fielding Smith added:

> "If a man cannot enter the kingdom of God without baptism, then the dead must be baptized. But how can they be baptized in water for the remission of their sins [when they are dead]? The only way it can be done is vicariously, someone who is living acting as a substitute for the dead."[243]

High ranking Mormon Milton R. Hunter said:

> "God… established on earth again the glorious doctrine of baptism for the dead, thereby opening the door to all of His sons and daughters who have ever lived in mortality to come back into His presence on condition of their worthiness."[244]

> "…the Lord has ordained baptism for the dead as the means whereby all his worthy children of all ages can become heirs of salvation in his kingdom… The millions who pass

---

242) Joseph Fielding Smith, *The Way to Perfection*, pp. 153-154.
243) Smith, *Doctrines of Salvation*, vol. 2, p. 141.
244) Hunter, *The Gospel Through the Ages*, p. 223.

to the spirit world without receiving an opportunity during mortality to hear the truths of salvation will receive their chance subsequent to what men call death... By accepting the gospel in the spirit world, and because the ordinances of salvation and exaltation are performed vicariously in this world, the worthy dead can become heirs of the fullness of the Father's kingdom..."[245]

"These are the principles in relation to the dead and the living... their salvation is necessary and essential to our salvation... they without us cannot be made perfect—neither can we without our dead be made perfect... there is a welding link of some kind or other between the fathers and the children... it is baptism for the dead. For we without them cannot be made perfect."[246]

What the Bible says:

"So then every one of us shall give account of himself to God." (Romans 14:12)

See also Isaiah 38:18, Psalm 49:7, Luke 16:26.

Secret 98

Mormon doctrine says baptism opens the door to personal sanctification:

"Baptism serves four purposes: 1. It is for remission of sins... 2. It admits the repentant

---

245) McConkie, *Mormon Doctrine*, pp. 73, 673.
246) Doctrine and Covenants 128:15,18.

person to membership in the Church and kingdom of God on earth... 3. It is the gate to the celestial kingdom of heaven, that is, it starts a person out on the straight and narrow path which leads to eternal life... 4. It is the means whereby the door to personal sanctification is opened."[247]

What the Bible says:

"For Christ sent me not to baptize, but to preach the gospel..." (1 Corinthians 1:17)

ADAM

Secret 99

Mormonism teaches that Adam and others helped Jesus form the earth:

"Adam and others helped in creation. It is true that Adam helped to form this earth. He labored with our Savior Jesus Christ. I have a strong view or conviction that there were others also who assisted them. Perhaps Noah and Enoch; and why not Joseph Smith..."[248]

What the Bible says:

"He [Jesus] was in the world, and the world was made by him, and the world knew him not." (John 1:10)

---

247) McConkie, *Mormon Doctrine*, p. 70.
248) Smith, *Doctrines of Salvation,* vol. 1, pp. 74-75.

Secret 100

Mormon doctrine says that Adam, not Jesus Christ, is the only begotten son of God:

"And in that day the Holy Ghost fell upon Adam, which beareth record of the Father and the Son, saying: I am the Only Begotten of the Father from the beginning, henceforth and forever, that as thou hast fallen thou mayest be redeemed, and all mankind, even as many as will."[249]

What the Bible says:

"And the Word [Jesus Christ] was made flesh, and dwelt among us, (and we beheld his glory, the glory as of the only begotten of the Father,) full of grace and truth." (John 1:14)

Secret 101

Mormon doctrine declares that Adam had to disobey God and fall into sin:

"…if Adam had not transgressed he would not have fallen… And they would have had no children… Adam fell that men might be…"[250]

"We are also informed in the scriptures that before Adam and Eve transgressed they were without children, and the fall was essen-

---

249) Pearl of Great Price, Moses 5:9.
250) Book of Mormon, 2 Nephi 2:22-23, 25.

tial to the peopling of the earth with their offspring."[251]

The following text is from the Mormon Temple Ceremony:

> "Eve (speaking): 'Do you not recollect that Father commanded us to multiply and replenish the earth? I have partaken of this fruit and by doing so shall be cast out, and you will be left a lone man in the Garden of Eden.'
>
> "Adam (speaking): 'Eve, I see that this must be so. I will partake that men may be.'
>
> "And in that day Adam blessed God... saying: Blessed be the name of God, for because of my transgression my eyes are opened, and in this life I shall have joy... And Eve, his wife, heard all these things and was glad, saying: Were it not for our transgression we never should have had seed, and never should have known good and evil..."[252]

What the Bible says:

It is NEVER good to sin. Genesis 3:12-19 details all of the the bad things that resulted from Adam's fall. Man, woman, the ground and the serpent were all cursed. Man's relationship with God was broken. Absolutely nothing good came from it.

---

251) Joseph Fielding Smith, *Answers to Gospel Questions,* vol. 1, p. 6.
252) Pearl of Great Price, Moses 5:10-11.

"For the wages of sin is death..." (Romans 6:23)

"...sin is a reproach to any people." (Proverbs 14:34)

Secret 102

Mormonism says Adam and Eve's fall wasn't really a sin:

"The fall of man came as a blessing in disguise... I never speak of the part Eve took in this fall as a sin, nor do I accuse Adam of a sin... It is not always a sin to transgress the law. This was a transgression of the law, but not a sin in the strict sense, for it was something that Adam and Eve had to do!" [253]

What the Bible says:

"Whosoever committeth sin transgresseth also the law: for sin is the transgression of the law." (1 John 3:4)

Secret 103

Mormonism teaches that when Adam fell, he fell upward:

"...Adam fell, but he fell in the right direction. He fell toward the goal... Adam fell, but he fell UPWARD..." [254]

What the Bible says:

"...sin, when it is finished, bringeth forth death." (James 1:15)

---

253) Smith, *Doctrines of Salvation,* vol. 1 pp. 114-115.
254) Sterling W. Sill (assistant to the council of the Twelve Apostles), Deseret News Church Section, July 31, 1965, p. 7.

Sin ALWAYS leads to destruction and death... it never leads upwards.

LUCIFER

Secret 104

Mormon doctrine says that Lucifer contested the appointment of Jesus to be the Saviour of the world.

> "The appointment of Jesus to be the Savior of the world was contested by one of the other sons of God. He was called Lucifer, son of the morning. Haughty, ambitious, and covetous of power and glory, this spirit-brother of Jesus desperately tried to become the Savior of mankind." [255]

> "...when the need for a Redeemer was explained, Satan offered to come into the world as the Son of God and be the Redeemer. 'Behold, here am I, send me,' he said, 'I wilt be thy son.' ...he sought to deny men their agency and to dethrone God. 'I will redeem all mankind, that one soul shall not be lost...'" [256]

Secret 105

Mormon doctrine says a "grand council" voted for Jesus, instead of Lucifer, to be the Saviour:

> "The contention in heaven was—Jesus said there would be certain souls that would not

---

255) Hunter, *The Gospel Through the Ages*, p. 15.
256) McConkie, *Mormon Doctrine*, pp. 192-193. See also Pearl of Great Price, Moses 4:1-3.

Secrets Mormons Don't Want You To Know

be saved; and the Devil said he could save them all, and laid down his plans before the grand council, who gave their vote in favor of Jesus Christ. So the Devil rose up in rebellion against God, and was cast down, with all who put their heads for him."[257]

What the Bible says:

The Bible says nothing about a "grand council" or a vote. God's word simply declares:

> "But when the fulness of the time was come, God sent forth his Son, made of a woman, made under the law, To redeem them that were under the law, that we might receive the adoption of sons." (Galatians 4:4-5)

Secret 106

Mormonism says Satan rebelled against God because his offer to redeem mankind was rejected by God:

> "With the rejection of his offer... Satan made open warfare against the Lord... 'A third part of the hosts of heaven' joined the rebellion; 'And they were thrust down, and thus came the devil and his angels...' Those thus cast out are denied bodies forever."[258]

What the Bible says:

The Bible says Satan rebelled against God because of his pride. He wanted to be like God:

---

257) *Journal of Discourses*, vol. 6, p. 8.
258) McConkie, *Mormon Doctrine*, pp. 192-193.

"How art thou fallen from heaven, O Lucifer, son of the morning! how art thou cut down to the ground, which didst weaken the nations! For thou hast said in thine heart, I will ascend into heaven, I will exalt my throne above the stars of God: I will sit also upon the mount of the congregation, in the sides of the north: I will ascend above the heights of the clouds; I will be like the most High." (Isaiah 14:12-14)

HELL

One word perfectly describes the Mormonism's belief about hell… "confusion," as these quotes show:

Secret 107

Some Mormons say there is no hell:

Mormon apostle John A. Widtsoe declared:

> "The meanest sinner will find some place in the heavenly realm… In the Church of Jesus Christ of Latter-day Saints, there is no hell. All will find a measure of salvation… The gospel of Jesus Christ has no hell in the old proverbial sense."[259]

What the Bible says:
> "…fear him which is able to destroy both soul and body in hell." (Matthew 10:28)

---

259) John A. Widtsoe, *Joseph Smith—Seeker After Truth,* pp. 177-178.

See also Psalm 9:17, Matthew 23:33, Mark 9:43, Luke 16:23-24, Isaiah 5:14; 14:9, Revelation 20:14-15.

Secret 108

Other Mormon documents claim that there is a hell:

> "When the wicked depart this life, they are 'cast out into outer darkness,' into hell, where 'they have no part nor portion of the Spirit of the Lord,' where they are spiritually dead. (Alma 40:13-14.) They remain spiritually dead in hell until the day of their resurrection (D. & C. 76:103-112), until 'death and hell' deliver up the dead which are in them, so that they may be judged according to their works." [260]

Secret 109

Mormonism says "eternal punishment" does NOT mean "punished eternally:"

> "Christians believed that to receive eternal punishment was to be punished eternally. This popular Christian error was corrected in a revelation." [261]

Former Mormon president Joseph Fielding Smith tries to explain that quote:

> "We learn from the Doctrine and Covenants that eternal punishment, or everlasting punishment, does not mean that a man

---

260) McConkie, *Mormon Doctrine,* p. 757.
261) Mormon historian B.H. Roberts, *Outlines of Ecclesiastical History,* p. 408.

condemned will endure this punishment forever."[262]

What the Bible says:
"And these shall go away into *everlasting* punishment: but the righteous into life eternal." (Matthew 25:46)

Secret 110

Mormonism teaches that people can escape from hell:

"Repentance opens the prison doors to the spirits in hell; it enables those bound with the chains of hell to free themselves from darkness, unbelief, ignorance, and sin. As rapidly as they can overcome these obstacles—gain light, believe truth, acquire intelligence, cast off sin, and break the chains of hell—they can leave the hell that imprisons them and dwell with the righteous in the peace of paradise."[263]

"Nevertheless, it is not written that there shall be no end to this torment…"[264]

What the Bible says:
"And beside all this, between us and you there is a great gulf fixed: so that they which would pass from hence to you cannot; neither can they pass to us, that would come from thence." (Luke 16:26)

---

262) Smith, *Doctrines of Salvation,* vol. 2, p. 160.
263) McConkie, *Mormon Doctrine,* p. 755.
264) Doctrine and Covenants 19:6.

Secret 111

Mormonism contradicts itself on the subject of hell having an end:

Doctrine and Covenants says:

> "Nevertheless, it is not written that there shall be no end to this torment." [265]

> "That part of the spirit world inhabited by wicked spirits who are awaiting the eventual day of their resurrection is called hell… Hell will have an end…" [266]

But the Book of Mormon says:

> "…not the destruction of the soul, save it be the casting of it into that hell which hath no end." (1 Nephi 14:3)

Secret 112

Mormonism teaches that "eternal" punishment can last as little as one hour:

> "Eternal punishment is God's punishment; everlasting punishment is God's punishment or in other words, it is the name of punishment God inflicts, he being eternal in nature. Whosoever, therefore, receives God's punishment receives eternal punishment, whether it be endured one hour, one week, one year, or an age." [267]

---

265) Doctrine and Covenants 19:6.
266) McConkie, *Mormon Doctrine*, pp. 349-350.
267) John Morgan, *The Plan of Salvation*, p. 30.

What the Bible says:

> "And the smoke of their torment ascendeth up *for ever and ever:* and they have no rest day nor night…" (Revelation 14:11)

See also Isaiah 66:24, Luke 16:26, Matthew 25:41.

TEMPLE GARMENTS

Secret 113

Special temple garments supposedly protect Mormons from Satan, temptation and evil:

Excerpt from the Mormon Temple Ceremony:

> "Brother (or Sister), having authority, I place this garment upon you, which you must wear throughout your life. It represents the garment given to Adam when he was found naked in the Garden of Eden, and is called the Garment of the Holy Priesthood. Inasmuch as you do not defile it, but are true and faithful to your covenants, it will be a shield and a protection to you against the power of the destroyer until you have finished your work here on earth."

From the First Presidency letter we read:

> "Wearing the garment is the sacred privilege of those who have taken upon themselves the covenants of the temple. The garment is a reminder of these covenants and, when prop-

erly worn, will serve as a protection against temptation and evil… This sacred covenant is between the member and the Lord and is an outward expression of an inner commitment to follow the Savior Jesus Christ."[268]

What the Bible says:
"…whoso putteth his trust in the LORD shall be safe." (Proverbs 29:25)

See also Psalm 118:8, Zechariah 4:6, Ephesians 6:11-17.

BIZARRE TEACHINGS OF BRIGHAM YOUNG

Secret 114

Brigham Young taught that Michael the Archangel brought Eve, one of his many wives, with him down to earth, and became Adam, our Father and our God:

"When our father Adam came into the garden of Eden, he came into it with a celestial body, and brought Eve, one of his wives, with him. He helped to make and organize this world. He is MICHAEL, the Archangel, the ANCIENT OF DAYS!… HE is our FATHER and our GOD, and the only God with whom WE have to do…"[269]

"…Jesus, our elder brother, was begotten in

---

268) The First Presidency letter, Nov. 5, 1996.
269) *Journal of Discourses*, vol. 1, pp. 50-51.

the flesh by the same character that was in the garden of Eden, and who is our Father in Heaven."[270]

"He (Adam) sat in the council of the gods in the planning of creation of this earth, and then, under Christ, participated in the creative enterprise… Father Adam… began his earth life as a son of God, endowed with the talents and abilities gained through diligence and obedience in pre-existence. He is the head of all gospel dispensations… the presiding high priest (under Christ) over all the earth; presides over all the spirits destined to inhabit this earth… holds the keys of salvation over all the earth; and will reign as Michael, our prince, to all eternity… He was baptized… married for eternity… He has returned to earth in our day, bringing keys and authorities to the Prophet Joseph Smith…"[271]

Brigham Young continued to teach this doctrine.

"Some have grumbled because I believe our God to be so near to us as Father Adam. There are many who know that doctrine to be true."[272]

In 1873, just a few years before he died, Brigham Young proclaimed:

---

270) *Journal of Discourses,* vol. 1, pp. 50-51.
271) McConkie, *Mormon Doctrine*, pp. 16-18.
272) *Journal of Discourses*, vol. 5, p. 331.

> "How much unbelief exists in the minds of the Latter-day Saints in regard to one particular doctrine which I revealed to them, and which God revealed to me-namely that Adam is our Father and God..." [273]

However, in 1976, Spencer W. Kimball, twelfth Prophet of the LDS church, denounced the Adam-God doctrine:

> "We warn you against the dissemination of doctrines which are alleged to have been taught by some of the General Authorities of past generations such for instance, is the Adam God theory. We denounce that theory and hope that everyone will be cautioned against this and other kinds of false doctrine." [274]

In 1980, Mormon Apostle Bruce McConkie declared:

> "There are those who believe, or say they believe, that Adam is our father and our God... The devil keeps this heresy alive... It is contrary to the whole plan of salvation... and anyone who has received the temple endowment and who yet believes the Adam-God theory does not deserve to be saved." [275]

What the Bible says:
> "Wherefore, as by one man {Adam} sin

---

273) *Desert News*, June 18, 1873.
274) *Church News*, October 9, 1976.
275) Mormon Apostle Bruce R. McConkie, speech given at the BYU Marriott Center, June 1, 1980.

entered into the world, and death by sin; and so death passed upon all men, for that all have sinned:" (Romans 5:12)

See also 1 Corinthians 15:22, Genesis 1:27; 2:7.

Secret 115

Brigham Young taught that every earth needs its own redeemer:

"Every earth has its redeemer, and every earth has its tempter; and every earth, and the people thereof, in their turn and time, receive all that we receive, and pass through all the ordeals that we are passing through." [276]

What the Bible says:

"To the only wise God our Saviour, be glory and majesty, dominion and power, both now and ever. Amen." (Jude 1:25)

Secret 116

Brigham Young taught that adulterers must be killed… by her nearest relative:

"The man who seduces his neighbors wife must die, and her nearest relative must kill him!" [277]

What the Bible says:

"…avenge not yourselves, but rather give place unto wrath: for it is written, Vengeance

---

276) *Journal of Discourses*, vol. 14, pp. 71-72.
277) Ibid., vol. 1, p. 97.

is mine; I will repay, saith the Lord."
(Romans 12:19)

Secret 117

Brigham Young taught that thieves should also be killed:

"I should be perfectly willing to see thieves have their throats cut."[278]

"If you want to know what to do with a thief that you may find stealing, I say kill him on the spot."[279]

What the Bible says:

"And be ye kind one to another, tenderhearted, forgiving one another, even as God for Christ's sake hath forgiven you."
(Ephesians 4:32)

Secret 118

Brigham Young taught that people live on the moon and sun:

"Who can tell us of the inhabitants of… the moon? …when you inquire about the inhabitants of that sphere you find that the most learned are as ignorant in regard to them as the most ignorant of their fellows. So it is with regard to the inhabitants of the sun. Do you think it is inhabited? I rather think it is. Do you think there is any life there? No question of it; it was not made in vain."[280]

---

278) Smith, *History of The Church*, vol. 7, p. 597.
279) *Journal of Discourses*, vol. 1, p. 108.
280) Ibid., vol. 13, p. 271.

Secret 119
Brigham Young believed that gold and silver grew like hair:

"Gold and silver grow, and so does every other kind of metal, the same as the hair upon my head, or the wheat in the field."[281]

Secret 120
Brigham Young claimed that every sermon he preached became scripture:

"I have never yet preached a sermon and sent it out to the children of men, that they may not call scripture."[282]

What the Bible says:

2 Timothy 3:16 says "All scripture is given by inspiration of God…" Obviously, God did not inspire Brigham Young to write that men live on the moon and gold and silver grow like hair.

SINS THAT DESERVE INSTANT DEATH

Secret 121
Mormon founders thought several sins deserve instant death:
MURDER:

"…even if a man kill another, I will shoot him, or cut off his head, spill his blood on

---
281) *Journal of Discourses*, vol. 1, p. 219.
282) Ibid., vol. 13, p. 95.

the ground, and let the smoke thereof ascend up to God..."[283]

ADULTERY AND IMMORALITY:

"Suppose you found your brother in bed with your wife, and put a javelin through both of them, you would be justified, and they would atone for their sins... I have no wife whom I love so well that I would not put a javelin through her heart, and I would do it with clean hands."[284]

SERIOUS SINS:

"Will you love your brothers or sisters likewise, when they have committed a sin that cannot be atoned for without the shedding of their blood? Will you love that man or woman well enough to shed their blood? ...I have known a great many men who have left this church for whom there is no chance whatever for exaltation, but if their blood had been spilled, it would have been better for them."[285]

STEALING:

"If you want to know what to do with a thief that you may find stealing, I say kill him on the spot..."[286]

---

283) Smith, *History of the Church,* vol. 5, p. 296.
284) *Journal of Discourses,* vol. 3, p. 247.
285) Ibid., vol. 4, pp. 219-220.
286) Ibid., vol. 1, p. 108.

MARRYING A BLACK PERSON:

"And if any man mingles his seed with the seed of Cane [sic] the only way he Could get rid of it or have salvation would be to Come forward and have his head cut off and spill his Blood upon the ground. It would also take the life of his Children."[287]

COVENANT BREAKING:

"…if they are covenant breakers we need a place designated, where we can shed their blood."[288]

LYING:

"I… warned those who lied and stole and followed Israel that they would have their heads cut off, for that was the law of God and it should be executed."[289]

What the Bible says:

"Jesus said, Thou shalt do no murder…" (Matthew 19:18)

"Thou knowest the commandments… Do not kill…" (Mark 10:19)

"Ye have heard that it was said by them of old time, Thou shalt not kill; and whosoever shall kill shall be in danger of the judgment:" (Matthew 5:21)

---

287) Brigham Young, Wilford Woodruffs Journal, vol. 4, p. 97.
288) *Journal of Discourses*, vol. 4, p. 50.
289) Brigham Young, *Manuscript History of Brigham Young,* Dec. 20, 1846.

POLYGAMY

Secret 122

Mormonism once taught that polygamy was an abomination:

"Behold, David and Solomon truly had many wives and concubines, which thing was abominable before me, saith the Lord."[290]

"Inasmuch as this Church of Christ has been reproached with the crime of fornication and polygamy; we declare that we believe that one man should have one wife; and one woman but one husband; except that in the event of death when either is at liberty to marry again."[291]

Secret 123

Mormon doctrine declares that those who are not polygamists are damned:

"Verily, thus saith the Lord unto you my servant Joseph… as touching the principle and doctrine of their having many wives and concubines… all those who have this law revealed unto them must obey the same. For behold, I reveal unto you a new and an everlasting covenant; and if ye abide not that covenant, then are ye damned; for no one can reject this covenant and be permitted to enter into my glory."[292]

---

290) Jacob 2:24.
291) The original Doctrine And Covenants 101:4 (1835 edition).
292) Doctrine and Covenants 132:1,3-4.

"Some people have supposed that the doctrine of plural marriage was a sort of superfluity, or nonessential to the salvation of mankind. In other words, some of the Saints have said, and believe, that a man with one wife… will receive an exaltation as great and glorious, if he is faithful, as he possibly could with more than one. I want here to enter my solemn protest against this idea, for I know it is false… I understand the law of celestial marriage to mean the every man in the Church, who has the ability to obey and practice it in righteousness and will not, shall be damned…"[293]

"I speak of plurality of wives as one of the most holy principles that God ever revealed to man, and all those who exercise an influence against it, unto whom it is taught, man or woman, will be damned, and they, and all who will be influenced by them, will suffer the buffetings of Satan in the flesh; for the curse of God will be upon them, and poverty, and distress, and vexation of spirit will be their portion;"[294]

"…the doctrine of plural and celestial marriage is the most holy and important doctrine ever revealed to man on earth, and that without obedience to that principle

---

293) *Journal of Discourses*, vol. 20, pp. 28, 31.
294) Ibid., vol. 11, p. 225

no man can ever attain to the fullness of exaltation in the celestial glory." [295]

"The principle of Plurality of Wives never will be done away." [296]

Wilford Woodruff said:

"The Lord will never give a revelation to abandon plural marriage." [297]

"Many of this people have broken their covenants by finding fault with the Plurality of Wives and trying to sink it out of existence. But you cannot do that. God will cut you off and raise up another people that will carry out his purposes in righteousness unless you walk up to the line in your duty." [298]

What the Bible says:

"Nevertheless, to avoid fornication, let every man have his own wife [not wives], and let every woman have her own husband [not husbands]." (1 Corinthians 7:2)

See also Genesis 2:24.

Secret 124

Mormonism teaches that to become a God, men MUST practice polygamy:

"The only men who become Gods, even

---

295) William Clayton, *Historical Record,* p. 266.
296) *Journal of Discourses,* vol. 3. p. 125.
297) Minutes of the Quorum of Twelve Apostles, 12 December, 1888.
298) *Journal of Discourses,* vol. 4. p. 108.

the Sons of God, are those who enter into polygamy."[299]

"Some people have supposed that the doctrine of plural marriage was a sort of superfluity, or nonessential to the salvation of mankind. In other words, some of the Saints have said, and believe, that a man with one wife… will receive an exaltation as great and glorious, if he is faithful, as he possibly could with more than one. I want here to enter my solemn protest against this idea, for I know it is false… Therefore, whoever has imagined that he could obtain the fullness of the blessings pertaining to this celestial law, by complying with only a portion of its conditions, has deceived himself. He cannot do it… I understand the law of celestial marriage to mean the every man in the Church, who has the ability to obey and practice it in righteousness and will not, shall be damned, I say I understand it to mean this and nothing less, and I testify in the name of Jesus that it does mean that."[300]

What the Bible says:

This is one lie built upon another. The Bible says nothing about men becoming Gods, so obviously it doesn't teach that sinning will get you there.

---

299) *Journal of Discourses*, vol. 11, p. 269.
300) Ibid., vol. 20, pp. 28, 31.

MARRIAGE FOR ETERNITY

Secret 125

Mormonism teaches that there are three major benefits of getting married in a Mormon temple:

1.) You will be married for eternity:

"Civil marriage makes servants in eternity... Celestial marriage makes Gods in eternity."[301]

2.) You will become a God:

"...if a man marry a wife by my word, which is my law, and by the new and everlasting covenant, and it is sealed unto them by the Holy Spirit of promise, by him who is anointed, unto whom I have appointed this power and the keys of this priesthood... Then shall they be gods, because they have no end; therefore shall they be from everlasting to everlasting..."[302]

3.) You will keep bearing children throughout eternity:

"'Except a man and his wife enter into an everlasting covenant and be married for eternity, while in this probation, by the power and authority of the holy priesthood,' The Prophet says, 'They will cease to increase when they die; that is, they will not have any children after the resurrection.'"[303]

---
301) Smith, *Doctrines of Salvation,* vol. 2, pp. 61-62.
302) Doctrine and Covenants 132:19-20.
303) McConkie, *Mormon Doctrine,* p. 238.

What the Bible says:
> "And Jesus answering said unto them, The children of this world marry, and are given in marriage: But they which shall be accounted worthy to obtain that world, and the resurrection from the dead, neither marry, nor are given in marriage:" (Luke 20:34-35)

> "…in the resurrection they neither marry, nor are given in marriage, but are as the angels of God in heaven." (Matthew 22:30)

See also Mark 12:25.

MORMONISM'S EVER-CHANGING NAME

Secret 126

The Mormon church claims to be the "only true church on the face of the earth."[304] One reason is because it has the name of Jesus Christ in its title.[305] They hold the name of their institution in high regard.

But when the LDS church officially started in 1830, it was called the "Church of Christ." This title supposedly came from Jesus Christ Himself.[306]

In 1834 the name was changed to the "Church of the

---
304) Doctrine and Covenants 1:30.
305) 17 Points of the True Church.
306) Whitmer, *An Address To All Believers In Christ,* p. 73.

Latter-Day Saints."[307] Then in 1838 it received its current name, "The Church of Jesus Christ of Latter-day Saints."[308]

If the name of the LDS church is as important as they claim, shouldn't the god of Mormonism have been able to get the title right the first time?

THE MASONRY CONNECTION

Secret 127

Joseph Smith was a high ranking Mason:

Joseph Smith himself admits:

"I officiated as grand chaplain at the installation of the Nauvoo Lodge of Free Masons, at the Grove near the Temple... In the evening I received the first degree in Freemasonry in the Nauvoo Lodge, assembled in my general business office.[309]

"I was with the Masonic Lodge and rose to the sublime degree."[310]

What the Bible says:

"And have no fellowship with the unfruitful works of darkness, but rather reprove them." (Ephesians 5:11)

---

307) Smith, *History of the Church,* vol. 2, p. 63.
308) Doctrine and Covenants 115:4.
309) Smith, *History of the Church,* vol. 4, p. 550-551.
310) Ibid., p. 552.

Secret 128
Many early Mormon leaders were Masons, including:
- Joseph Smith, Sr. (Joseph Smith's father.)
- Hyrum, Samuel, and William Smith (Joseph Smith's three brothers.)
- Brigham Young (Mormonism's second president.)
- John Taylor (Mormonism's third president.)
- Wilford Woodruff (Mormonism's fourth president.)
- Lorenzo Snow (Mormonism's fifth president.)
- Sidney Rigdon (Counselor to Joseph Smith).
- John C. Bennett (Assistant president to the First Presidency).
- Heber C. Kimball (first counselor to Brigham Young.)
- Willard Richards (second counselor to Brigham Young.)
- Newell K. Whitney (Presiding Bishop).
- Orson Pratt, Parley P. Pratt, Orson Hyde, Lyman Johnson and Erastus Snow (Mormon apostles.)
- William Law (second counselor to Joseph Smith).
- Orrin Porter Rockwell (Joseph Smith's bodyguard)
- William Clayton (Joseph Smith's secretary)
- William Marks (Nauvoo Stake president).

What the Bible says:
> "A good tree cannot bring forth evil fruit, neither can a corrupt tree bring forth good fruit." (Matthew 7:18)

Secret 129

Joseph Smith added Masonic rituals to the Mormon religion:

Joseph Smith received his first degree in Masonry on March 15, 1842, and the very next day was elevated to the degree of Sublime Master of the Royal Secret.[311]

> "Six weeks later, on May 2, 1842, Smith was teaching these Masonic secrets as his own 'revelations' to Mormon leaders as the temple Endowment."[312]

It was from the Masons that Joseph Smith invented the basic ceremonies and symbols that are now known as the Endowment.

> "Into the fabric of Freemasonry he wove his own peculiar brand of occultism, claiming it to be 'revelation' from on high."[313]

Mormon historian Reed C. Durham, Jr. wrote:

> "There is absolutely no question in my mind that the Mormon ceremony which came to be known as the Endowment, introduced by Joseph Smith to Mormon Masons initially, just a little over one month after he became a Mason, had an immediate inspiration from Masonry."[314]

The outside of the Temple in Salt Lake City has

---
311) *Documented History of the Church*, vol. 4, pp. 550, 552.
312) Ibid., vol. 5, p. 2.
313) W.J. McCormick, *Christ, the Christian, and Freemasonry*, Belfast: Great Joy Publications, 1984; p. 96.
314) Reed C. Durham, Jr., *No Help For the Widow's Son*, 1980, p. 17.

many Masonic designs, like the All-Seeing Eye, the inverted 5-pointed star, and the clasped hands or grip. Each of these were part of Masonry before Joseph Smith started using them.

What the Bible says:
> "Wherefore by their fruits ye shall know them." (Matthew 7:20)

MORMON PROPHETS

Secret 130
Mormonism claims that their prophet is God's mouthpiece, who makes salvation available:

> "Upon the president of the Church the Almighty bestows the highest office and the greatest gifts that mortal man is capable of receiving… He is the one man on earth at a time who can hold and exercise the keys of the kingdom in their fulness… By the authority vested in him, all ordinances of the gospel are performed, all teaching of the truths of salvation is authorized, and through the keys which he holds, salvation itself is made available to men of this day. The President of the Church is the mouthpiece of God on earth." [315]

"Brethren, keep your eye on the President of

---
315) McConkie, *Mormon Doctrine*, pp. 591-592.

the church. If he tells you anything and it is wrong and you do it, the Lord will bless you for it. But you don't need to worry: the Lord will not let his mouthpiece lead this people astray."[316]

What the Bible says:
"Then the LORD said unto me, The prophets prophesy lies in my name: I sent them not, neither have I commanded them, neither spake unto them: they prophesy unto you a false vision and divination, and a thing of nought, and the deceit of their heart." (Jeremiah 14:14)

Secret 131

Mormonism claims that salvation is contingent upon obeying the words of their prophet:

"Our salvation is contingent upon our belief in a living prophet and adherence to his word. He alone has the right to revelation for the whole church…"[317]

What the Bible says:

Salvation is contingent upon faith in Jesus Christ, not obedience to a sinful man.

"For I am not ashamed of the gospel of Christ: for it is the power of God unto salvation to every one that believeth; to the Jew first, and also to the Greek." (Romans 1:16)

---
316) Heber J. Grant, Ensign Magazine, October 1972, p. 7.
317) Theodore A. Tuttle, Deseret News, April 7, 1973, p. 11.

Secret 132

Mormonism's claim: everything the Mormon prophet says is scripture:

> "...the greatest of all scripture we have today is current scripture. What a mouthpiece of God says today is scripture."[318]

> "...thou shalt give heed unto all his words and commandments which he shall give unto you as he receiveth them, walking in all holiness before me; For his word ye shall receive, as if from mine own mouth, in all patience and faith."[319]

What the Bible says:

> "If any man think himself to be a prophet, or spiritual, let him acknowledge that the things that I write unto you are the commandments of the Lord." (1 Corinthians 14:37)

We do not need prophets to communicate God's Word to us today because we have the complete Word of God in the King James version of the Bible.

> "God, who at sundry times and in divers manners spake in time past unto the fathers by the prophets, Hath in these last days spoken unto us by his Son, whom he hath appointed heir of all things, by whom also he made the worlds;" (Hebrews 1:1-2)

---

318) Theodore A. Tuttle, Deseret News, April 7, 1973, p. 11.
319) Doctrine and Covenants 21:4-5.

DO MORMON LEADERS HATE CHRISTIANITY?

Secret 133

Book of Mormon:

"Behold there are save two churches only; the one is the Church of the Lamb of God [i.e.. the Mormon Church] and the other is the church of the devil [i.e.. the Christian Church]; wherefore whosoever belongeth not to the church of the lamb of God belongeth to that great church; which is the mother of abominations; and she is the whore of all the earth." [320]

Brigham Young:

(Second prophet of the Mormon church)

"The Christian world, so called, are heathens as to their knowledge of the salvation of God." [321]

"With regard to true theology a more ignorant people never lived than the present so-called Christian world." [322]

"When the light came to me I saw that all the so-called Christian world was grovelling in darkness." [323]

---

320) The Book of Mormon, 1 Nephi 14:10.
321) *Journal of Discourses*, vol. 8, p. 171.
322) Ibid., vol. 8, p. 199.
323) Ibid., vol. 5, p. 73.

"…he that confesseth not that Jesus has come in the flesh and sent Joseph Smith with the fullness of the Gospel to this generation, is not of God, but is anti-christ."[324]

John Taylor:

(Third prophet of the Mormon church)

"Christianity… is a perfect pack of nonsense… it is as corrupt as hell; and the Devil could not invent a better engine to spread his work than the Christianity of the nineteenth century."[325]

"What! are Christians ignorant? Yes, as ignorant of the things of God as the brute beast."[326]

Orson Pratt:

(Mormon apostle)

"Both Catholics and Protestants are nothing less than the 'whore of Babylon' whom the Lord denounces by the mouth of John the Revelator as having corrupted all the earth by their fornications and wickedness. Any person who shall be so corrupt as to receive a holy ordinance of the Gospel from the ministers of any of these apostate churches will be sent down to hell with them, unless they repent."[327]

---

324) *Journal of Discourses*, vol. 9, p. 312.
325) Ibid., vol. 6, p. 167.
326) Ibid., vol. 13, p. 225.
327) Pratt, *The Seer*, p. 255.

Bruce McConkie:
> "Believers in the doctrines of modern Christendom will reap damnation to their souls."[328]

What the Bible says:
> "Beware of false prophets, which come to you in sheep's clothing, but inwardly they are ravening wolves." (Matthew 7:15)

MORMON TEMPLES

Secret 134

Mormonism teaches that temples are required to administer secret ordinances:
> "Certain gospel ordinances are of such a sacred and holy nature that the Lord authorizes their performance only in holy sanctuaries prepared and dedicated for that very purpose... Baptism for the dead... is a temple ordinance, an ordinance of salvation. All other temple ordinances—washings, anointings, endowments, sealings—pertain to exaltation within the celestial kingdom... All of these ordinances of exaltation are performed in the temples for both the living and the dead... They were given in modern times to the Prophet Joseph Smith by revelation..."[329]

---
328) McConkie, *Mormon Doctrine*, p. 177.
329) Ibid., p. 779.

What the Bible says:
> "Howbeit the most High dwelleth not in temples made with hands; as saith the prophet, Heaven is my throne, and earth is my footstool: what house will ye build me?"
> (Acts 7:48-49)

Temples are not necessary today. During the Old Testament, they were used for the animal sacrifices that covered the people's sins. When Jesus was crucified, the veil of the temple was rent from top to bottom, signifying an end to the Old Testament sacrifices, since Jesus became our final atoning sacrifice.

See also 2 Chronicles 2:6, Acts 17:24, Revelation 21:22.

MORMON CONTRADICTIONS

Secret 135

Mormonism contradicts the Bible and its own documents:

1. The Book of Mormon says God is a "Spirit"[330] but other Mormon teaching says he has "a body of flesh and bones."[331]

2. The Book of Mormon says "...the decrees of God are unalterable..."[332] but Doctrine and Covenants 56:4 says, "I, the Lord, command and revoke as it seemeth me good..."

---

330) Book of Mormon, Alma 18:26, Alma 22:8-10
331) Doctrine and Covenants 130:22; Smith, *Teachings of the Prophet Joseph Smith*, p. 345; *Journal of Discourses*, vol. 7, p. 333.
332) Book of Mormon, Alma 41:8.

3. The Pearl of Great Price says "…there is no God beside me…"[333] But in 1938, Joseph Fielding Smith declared that you must "…learn how to be God's yourselves, and to be kings and priests to God, the same as all gods have done before you."[334]

4. Mormon scripture says, "For behold, God knowing all things, being from everlasting to everlasting…"[335] Yet the founder of the religion contradicts that,

> "We have imagined and supposed that God was God from all eternity. I will refute that idea and take away the veil, so that you may see… he was once a man like us…"[336]

5. One Mormon scripture states:

> "…the Lord hath said that he dwelleth not in unholy temples, but in the hearts of the righteous doth he dwell…"[337]

But another Mormon scripture teaches:

> "…the idea that the Father and the Son dwell in a man's heart is an old sectarian notion, and is false."[338]

---

333) Pearl of Great Price, Moses 1:6. See also Book of Mormon, Alma 11:27-29, 38-39; Book of Mormon, 2 Nephi 31:21, Book of Mormon, Alma 11:44, Book of Mormon, 3 Nephi 11:27; Doctrine and Covenants 20:28.
334) Smith, *Teachings of the Prophet Joseph Smith*, pp. 346-347. See also Doctrine and Covenants 132:20; Pearl of Great Price, Abraham 4:1,18; 5:20.
335) Book of Mormon, Moroni 7:22; 8:18, Doctrine and Covenants 20:12, Book of Mormon, 3 Nephi 24:6.
336) Smith, *Teachings of The Prophet Joseph Smith,* pp. 345-346.
337) Book of Mormon, Alma 34:36.
338) Doctrine and Covenants 130:3.

6. The Book of Mormon plainly states:

> "Mary… shall be overshadowed and conceived by the power of the Holy Ghost…"[339]

> "And behold, he shall be born of Mary… who shall be overshadowed and conceived by the power of the Holy Ghost…"[340]

But Mormonism also teaches:

> "Christ was begotten by an Immortal Father in the same way that mortal men are begotten by mortal fathers…"[341]

7. Genesis 5:23 says Enoch was 365 years old when God took him to heaven, but Doctrine and Covenants 107:49 contradicts the Bible, saying he was 430 years old when he was translated.

8. Mormon scripture says Jesus was born in Jerusalem,"[342] but the Bible says He was born in Bethlehem."[343]

9. One Mormon scripture teaches that man did NOT pre-exist by saying that "man in the beginning was created after the image of God,[344] while another Mormon scripture says Man DID pre-exist: "Man was also in the beginning with God."[345]

---

339) Book of Mormon, Alma 7:10.
340) Ibid.
341) McConkie, *Mormon Doctrine,* pp. 547, 742.
342) Book of Mormon, Alma 7:10.
343) Matthew 2:1. See also Micah 5:2, Luke 2:4, 11.
344) Book of Mormon, Alma 18:34.
345) Doctrine and Covenants 93:29

THE SPIRIT WORLD

Secret 136

Mormonism teaches that before being born on earth, we are born and grow up in the spirit world as the spirit children of God and one of His wives, possessing divine attributes inherited from our Heavenly Father and Mother:

"Before we were born we lived with our Heavenly Father and Heavenly Mother. We were their spirit children."[346]

"We forget that we have a Heavenly Father and a Heavenly Mother who are even more concerned, probably, than our earthly father and mother…"[347]

"in the former life we were spirits."[348]

"in the first stage, man was an eternally existent being termed an intelligence. In that sphere of existence each individual was naturally conscious… The next realm where man dwelt was the spirit world… numerous sons and daughters were begotten and born of heavenly parents into that eternal family in the spirit world. In the likeness of God Himself, these spirit children were organized, possessing divine, eternal, and godlike attributes, inherited from their Heavenly Father and Mother. There in the spirit world they

---
346) Marilynne T. Lindford, *ABC's for Young LDS*, p. 6.
347) Quotations from President Harold B. Lee," *Ensign*, Feb. 1974.
348) Smith, *Doctrines of Salvation,* vol. 1, p. 57.

were reared to maturity, becoming grown spirit men and women prior to coming upon this earth."[349]

"Our spirit bodies had their beginning in pre-existence when we were born as the spirit children of God our Father. Through that birth process spirit element was organized into intelligent entities. The bodies so created have all the parts of mortal bodies... We had spirit bodies in pre–existence..."[350]

What the Bible says:

This is a totally unbiblical Mormon doctrine.

Secret 137

Mormonism teaches that we are literal children of God, not spiritual sons and daughters:

"...the Gods were to be parents of spirit children just as our Heavenly Father and Heavenly Mother were the parents of the people of this earth."[351]

"Our spirit bodies had their beginning in pre–existence when we were born as the spirit children of God our Father... All men in pre–existence were the spirit children of God our Father, an exalted, glorified, and perfected Man."[352]

---

349) Hunter, *The Gospel Through the Ages*, p. 127.
350) McConkie, *Mormon Doctrine*, pp. 750-751.
351) Hunter, *The Gospel Through the Ages*, p. 120.
352) McConkie, *Mormon Doctrine*, pp. 750-751.

> "The Father of Jesus is our Father also... Jesus, however is the Firstborn among all the sons of God... He is our elder brother... All men and women are in the similitude of the universal Father and Mother, and are literally the sons and daughters of Deity... man, as a spirit, was begotten and born of heavenly parents... Man is the child of God, formed in the divine image and endowed with divine attributes, and even as the infant son of an earthly father and mother is capable in due time of becoming a man, so the undeveloped offspring of celestial parentage is capable, by experience through ages and aeons, of evolving into a God."[353]

What the Bible says:

We are all God's *creation*, but we are not all His *children*. We are by nature the children of wrath (Ephesians 2:3) and are dead in trespasses and sins (Ephesians 2:1). We become God's child only through faith in Jesus Christ:

> "But as many as received him, to them gave he power to become the sons of God, even to them that believe on his name:" (John 1:12)

> "Having predestinated us unto the adoption of children by Jesus Christ to himself..." (Ephesians 1:5)

See also Galatians 3:26; 4:5.

---

353) Joseph Fielding Smith, *Man: His Origin and Destiny,* pp. 351, 354-355.

Secret 138

Mormonism teaches that animals, fish and plants all existed as spirit entities before they were created on the earth:

"Animals, fowls, fishes, plants, and all forms of life were first created as distinct spirit entities in pre-existence before they were created 'naturally upon the face of the earth.' That is, they lived as spirit entities before coming to this earth; they were spirit animals, spirit birds, and so forth… All men in pre-existence were the spirit children of God our Father, an exalted, glorified, and perfected Man."[354]

What the Bible says:

Another totally unbiblical Mormon doctrine.

MORMON TEACHINGS ABOUT MAN

Secret 139

Mormonism teaches that man always existed:

"Man was also in the beginning with God. Intelligence, or the light of truth, was not created or made, neither indeed can be."[355]

"All the fools and learned and wise men from the beginning of creation, who say that the spirit of man had a beginning, prove that it

---

354) McConkie, *Mormon Doctrine*, pp. 750-751.
355) Doctrine and Covenants 93:29.

must have an end; and if that doctrine is true, then the doctrine of annihilation would be true. But if I am right, I might with boldness proclaim from the house–tops that God never had the power to create the spirit of man at all. God himself could not create himself. Intelligence is eternal and exists upon a self–existent principle."[356]

"That matter or element is self–existent and eternal in nature, creation being merely the organization and reorganization of that substance... and if there had been no self–existent spirit element, there would have been no substance from which those spirit bodies could have been organized."[357]

"In the former life we were spirits."[358]

What the Bible says:

"So God created man in his own image, in the image of God created he him; male and female created he them." (Genesis 1:27)

"And the LORD God formed man of the dust of the ground, and breathed into his nostrils the breath of life; and man became a living soul." (Genesis 2:7)

See also Isaiah 44:2, Psalm 139:14, Ephesians 2:10, Zechariah 12:1.

---

356) Smith, *Teachings of the Prophet Joseph Smith,* p. 354.
357) McConkie, *Mormon Doctrine,* p. 589.
358) Smith, *Doctrines of Salvation,* vol. 1, p. 57.

Secret 140

Mormonism teaches that man is not born with a sin nature:

"...modern Christendom has the false doctrine of original sin."[359]

"...wherefore, little children are whole, for they are not capable of committing sin..."[360]

"Children who develop normally become accountable when 'eight years old...'"[361]

What the Bible says:

"Behold, I was shapen in iniquity; and in sin did my mother conceive me." (Psalm 51:5)

See also Ecclesiastes 7:20, James 2:10, Romans 3:23; 6:23, 1 John 1:8.

A thought: Why are kids baptized at age 8 for remission of sins if they aren't accountable for any sin until age 8?

MORE STRANGE MORMON TEACHINGS

Secret 141

Orson Pratt taught that vegetables have living spirits and are capable of feeling, knowing and rejoicing:

"The spirit of a vegetable is in the same image and likeness of its tabernacle, and of the same

---

359) McConkie, *Mormon Doctrine*, p. 550.
360) Book of Mormon, Moroni 8:8.
361) McConkie, *Mormon Doctrine*, p. 853.

magnitude, for it fills every part thereof. It is capable of existing in an organized form before it enters its vegetable house, and also after it departs from it. If the spirit of an apple tree were rendered visible when separated from its natural tabernacle, it would appear in the form, likeness, and magnitude of the natural apple tree; and so it is with the spirit of every other tree, or herb, or blade of grass, its shape, its magnitude, and its appearance, resemble the natural tabernacle intended for its residence… When the spiritual vegetable withdraws, the natural one decays and returns to its original elements; but its spirit, being a living substance, remains in its organized form, capable of happiness in its own sphere, and will again inherit a celestial tabernacle when all things are made new… we are compelled to believe that every vegetable, whether great or small, has a living intelligent spirit capable of feeling, knowing, and rejoicing in its sphere." [362]

Secret 142

Orson Pratt claimed that eternal life could be obtained by eating "celestial vegetables:"

"The celestial vegetables and fruits which grow out of the soil of this redeemed Heaven, constitute the food of the Gods. This food differs from the food derived from the veg-

---

362) Pratt, *The Seer*, pp. 33-34.

etables of a fallen world: the latter... produces flesh and bones of a mortal nature... while the former, or celestial vegetables, are, when digested in the stomach, converted into a fluid, which, in its nature, is spiritual, and which, circulating in the veins and arteries of the celestial male and female, preserves their tabernacles from decay and death. Earthly vegetables form blood, and blood forms flesh and bones; celestial vegetables, when digested, form a spiritual fluid which gives immortality and eternal life..." [363]

What the Bible says:
"That whosoever believeth in him should not perish, but have eternal life." (John 3:15)

Secret 143

Mormon doctrine says it's unsafe to travel on water because God has cursed the waters:

"For I, the Lord, have decreed in mine anger many destructions upon the waters; yea, and especially upon these waters." [364]

"Behold, I, the Lord, in the beginning blessed the waters; but in the last days, by the mouth of my servant John, I cursed the waters..." [365]

What the Bible says:
Another bizarre unbiblical Mormon doctrine.

---

363) Pratt, *The Seer.*, p. 37.
364) Doctrine and Covenants 61:5.
365) Ibid. 61:14-15.

Secret 144

Mormonism teaches that earth was conceived by its parent earths:

"Does the earth conceive? It does, and it brings forth. ...Where did the earth come from? From its parent earths." [366]

What the Bible says:

"For thus saith the LORD that created the heavens; God himself that formed the earth and made it; he hath established it, he created it..." (Isaiah 45:18)

Secret 145

Mormonism teaches that earth will eventually die and be resurrected as a celestial sphere:

"...this earth was created first as a spirit, and that it was thereafter clothed upon with tangible, physical element... It was created (the equivalent of birth); it fell to its present mortal or telestial state; it was baptized by immersion, when the universal flood swept over its entire surface... it will be baptized by fire... it will die; and finally it will be quickened (or resurrected) and become a celestial sphere." [367]

What the Bible says:

The Bible says nothing about the earth dying, being "resurrected" or becoming a "celestial sphere."

---

366) *Journal of Discourses*, vol. 6, p. 36.
367) McConkie, *Mormon Doctrine*, pp. 210-211, 251-252.

Secret 146

Mormonism teaches members how to tell if they are face to face with the devil:

"If it be the devil as an angel of light, when you ask him to shake hands he will offer you his hand, and you will not feel anything; you may therefore detect him." [368]

What the Bible says:

More Mormon doctrine not taught in the Bible.

Secret 147

Mormonism teaches that spirits must be compressed so they can fit inside infant bodies:

"A great many people have supposed that the spirit which exists in the tabernacle, for instance, of an infant, is of the same size as the infant tabernacle when it enters therein. No one will dispute that it is of the same size when it is enclosed therein; but how large was the spirit before it entered the tabernacle?… When all these spirits were sent forth from the eternal worlds, they were, no doubt, not infants; but when they entered the infant tabernacle, they were under the necessity… of being *compressed*, or diminished in size so that their spirits could be enclosed in infant tabernacles…" [369]

---

368) Doctrine and Covenants 129:8.
369) *Journal of Discourses*, vol. 16, pp. 333-334.

What the Bible says:

The Bible says nothing about spirits being compressed.

Secret 148

Mormonism teaches that compressed spirits cause the loss of wisdom and knowledge:

"When Jesus was born into our world, his previous knowledge was taken from Him: this was occasioned by His spiritual body being compressed into a smaller volume than it originally occupied… when this spirit was compressed, so as to be wholly enclosed in an infant tabernacle, it had a tendency to suspend the memory; and the wisdom and knowledge, formerly enjoyed, were forgotten… So it is with man. When he enters a body of flesh, his spirit is so compressed and contracted in infancy that he forgets his former existence…"[370]

What the Bible says:

Here, one falsehood is built on top of another falsehood. The Bible never mentions this.

Secret 149

More bizarre Mormon doctrines about spirit bodies:

"When a baby dies, it goes back into the spirit world, and the spirit assumes its natural form as an adult, for we were all adults before

---

370) Pratt, *The Seer,* p. 21.

we were born. When a child is raised in the resurrection, the spirit will enter the body and the body will be the same size as it was when the child died. It will then grow after the resurrection to full maturity to conform to the size of the spirit."[371]

Secret 150

Mormon doctrine says the sin of murder cannot be forgiven:

"And now, behold, I speak unto the church. Thou shalt not kill; and he that kills shall not have forgiveness in this world, nor in the world to come."[372]

What the Bible says:

"…the blood of Jesus Christ his Son cleanseth us from all sin." (1 John 1:7)

Secret 151

Mormonism says angels are "resurrected personages:"

"There are two kinds of beings in heaven, namely: Angels, who are resurrected personages, having bodies of flesh and bones…"[373]

What the Bible says:

"Thou, even thou, art LORD alone; thou hast made heaven, the heaven of heavens, with all their host…" (Nehemiah 9:6)

---

371) Smith, *Doctrines of Salvation*, vol. 2, p. 56.
372) Doctrine and Covenants 42:18.
373) Ibid. 129:1.

Secret 152

Mormons are taught to trust their feelings rather than facts:

"But, behold, I say unto you, that you must study it out in your mind; then you must ask me if it be right, and if it is right I will cause that your bosom shall burn within you; therefore, you shall feel that it is right." [374]

What the Bible says:

"The heart is deceitful above all things, and desperately wicked: who can know it?" (Jeremiah 17:9)

See also 1 Thessalonians 5:21, 2 Timothy 2:15, Matthew 22:29, Proverbs 14:12; 16:25.

Secret 153

Mormons are ordered to obey their leaders… right or wrong:

The Journal of Discourse commands Mormons to:

"…learn to do as you are told… if you are told by your leader to do a thing, do it. None of your business whether it is right or wrong." [375]

"Any Latter-day Saint who denounces or opposes, whether actively or otherwise, any plan or doctrine advocated by the 'prophets, seers, and revelators' of the Church is cultivating the spirit of apostasy… Lucifer… wins a great victory when he can get members of the

---

[374] Doctrine and Covenants 9:8.
[375] *Journal of Discourses,* vol. 6, p. 32.

> Church to speak against their leaders and to 'do their own thinking.' …When our leaders speak, the thinking has been done. When they propose a plan, it is God's plan. When they point the way, there is no other which is safe. When they give direction, it should mark the end of controversy."[376]

> "The Lord will never permit me or any other man who stands as the President of this Church to lead you astray. It is not in the program."[377]

Back when Mormons were taught the ridiculous lie that Adam was God, Mormon Elder James A. Little declared:

> "I believe in the principle of obedience; and if I am told that Adam is our Father and our God, I just believe it."[378]

What the Bible says:
> "Thus saith the LORD; Cursed be the man that trusteth in man, and maketh flesh his arm, and whose heart departeth from the LORD." (Jeremiah 17:5)

> "Beloved, believe not every spirit, but try the spirits whether they are of God: because many false prophets are gone out into the world." (1 John 4:1)

---

376) Improvement ERA, 1945, p. 354.
377) Wilford Woodruff, *Essentials in Church History*, p. 609.
378) *Millennial Star*, vol. 16, p. 530.

Secret 154

Mormonism teaches that Mary had two husbands:

"The man Joseph, the husband of Mary, did not, that we know of, have more than one wife, but Mary the wife of Joseph had another husband." [379]

What the Bible says:

Nothing in the Bible or history suggests this is true.

Secret 155

Mormonism teaches that some people can't repent:

"No one can repent on the cross, nor in prison, nor in custody." [380]

What the Bible says:

The Lord said to the thief on the cross next to Him:

"To day shalt thou be with me in paradise." (Luke 23:43)

Secret 156

Mormonism says death-bed repentance is vain:

"Hopes of reward through so-called death-bed repentance are vain." [381]

What the Bible says:

"...him that cometh to me I will in no wise cast out." (John 6:37)

---

379) Jerald and Sandra Tanner, *The Changing World of Mormonism*, p. 180, quoting Deseret News, Young, October 10, 1866.
380) Kimball, *The Miracle of Forgiveness*, p. 167.
381) McConkie, *Mormon Doctrine*, p. 631.

Secret 157

Mormonism teaches that in eternity Cain will rule over Satan:

"...he became the first mortal to be cursed as a son of perdition. As a result of his mortal birth he is assured of a tangible body of flesh and bones in eternity, a fact which will enable him to rule over Satan."[382]

What the Bible says:

Another completely unbiblical Mormon doctrine.

Secret 158

The Book of Mormon's math problem:

In Ether 6, the Book of Mormon says Jared and his brother boarded barges headed for the "promised land." The Lord supposedly caused a "furious wind" to blow for 344 days, which delivered them to their destination.

But even if this "furious wind" blew only 10 m.p.h. they would have sailed 82,560 miles, and circled the globe more than three times.

Secret 159

Mormon president: "lying for the Lord?"

In a 1997 newspaper interview, Gordon Hinckley, president of the Mormon church, was asked "...don't Mormons believe that God was once a man?" Hinckley replied:

"I wouldn't say that... That gets into some

---

382) McConkie, *Mormon Doctrine*, pp. 108-109.

pretty deep theology that we don't know very much about."[383]

Less than four months later, Hinkley answered the same question in TIME magazine:

"I don't know that we teach it. I don't know that we emphasize it... I understand the philosophical background behind it, but I don't know a lot about it, and I don't think others know a lot about it."[384]

Was Gordon Hinckley lying? Or was the President of the Mormon religion really unfamiliar with this central doctrine of Mormonism that has been taught by Mormons ever since Joseph Smith declared that God was "once a man like us."[385]

You must answer that question for yourself.

Secret 160

The Book of Mormon's promise to American Indians was dropped because it never came true:

The Book of Mormon used to promise American Indians that when they accepted the Mormon gospel, their skin would turn "white" and delightsome.

"...many generations shall not pass away among them, save they shall be a *white* and a delightsome people."[386]

---

383) San Francisco Chronicle, April 13, 1997, p. 3/Z1
384) TIME magazine, August 4, 1997, p. 56.
385) Smith, *Teachings of the Prophet Joseph Smith,* pp. 345-346.
386) Book of Mormon, 2 Nephi 30:6, 1830 edition, p. 117.

Since this never happened, in 1981 the text was changed to "pure" and delightsome:

> "...and many generations shall not pass away among them, save they shall be a *pure* and a delightsome people."[387]

Secret 161
The National Geographic Society says the Mormon religion makes false claims about the Book of Mormon:

The following is from a letter from the National Geographic Society that refutes Mormon claims about the Book of Mormon:

> "I referred your inquiry to Dr. George Stuart, the staff archaeologist of the Society. He informed me that neither the Society nor any other institution of equal prestige has ever used the Book of Mormon in locating archaeological sites. Although many Mormon sources claim that the Book of Mormon has been substantiated by archaeological findings, this claim has not been verified scientifically."[388]

Secret 162
Mormonism falsely claims that the Smithsonian Institute uses the Book of Mormon in archaeological research:

> "Your recent inquiry concerning the Smithsonian Institution's alleged use of the Book of Mormon as a scientific guide has been

---
387) Book of Mormon, 2 Nephi 30:6, 1981 edition.
388) National Geographic Society, letter dated February 4, 1982.

received in the Smithsonian's Department of Anthropology.

"The Book of Mormon is a religious document and not a scientific guide. The Smithsonian Institution does not use it in archeological research. Because the Smithsonian Institution receives many inquiries regarding the Book of Mormon, we have prepared a 'Statement Regarding the Book of Mormon...'

"1. The Smithsonian Institution has never used the Book of Mormon in any way as a scientific guide. Smithsonian archeologists see no direct connection between the archeology of the New World and the subject matter of the book."[389]

---

389) "Statement Regarding the Book of Mormon," Smithsonian Institution, 1986.

WHY WE LEFT THE MORMON CHURCH

Of all the millions of people in the world, I held it a privilege to be one of those born into a Mormon home.

I cherished my Mormon heritage, thinking I was very special to God because he had placed me into a family who belonged to "the only true church"[390] and I knew this put me ahead of many people in my advancement towards becoming a goddess, along with my husband becoming a god over our own world.[391]

I started attending the LDS church as an infant and received my name and blessing by the hand of my father when I was three months old. The only religious training I had was the teachings of the Church of Jesus Christ of Latter-day Saints.

---

390) Doctrine and Covenants 1:30; McConkie, *Mormon Doctrine,* p. 136.
391) McConkie, *Mormon Doctrine*, pp. 613, 844; *Journal of Discourses*, vol. 3, p. 93; Smith, *Teachings of the Prophet Joseph Smith*, p. 346.

As a Mormon, I was taught that there were millions of gods, but we served the God of this world, whose name is Elohim,[392] who lived near the planet Kolob.[393]

We were taught he was once a mortal man who, through obedience to Mormon laws and ordinances, was exalted to the status of godhood,[394] just like his father before him, and his father before him, to eternity past.[395]

Elohim is a polygamist.[396] The number of wives he has is unknown. These wives bore to him billions of spirit babies. These spiritual children lived with him and his wives in a pre-existent realm.

We were taught that the pre-existence was a place where every human being born on earth lived as one of these spirit children.[397] Elohim saw that his children needed to advance farther, so he decided it was time for them to take a physical body upon the earth to undergo the experiences of mortality.

Thus, Elohim called together a council of the gods to decide the destiny of all those who would be sent to earth. Two of Elohim's sons were there: Jehovah (the first born and the Mormon Jesus) and Lucifer.

---

392) McConkie, *Mormon Doctrine*, p. 224.
393) Pearl of Great Price, Abraham 3:2-3; McConkie, *Mormon Doctrine*, p. 428.
394) Smith, *Teachings of the Prophet Joseph Smith*, p. 345; Hunter, *Gospel Through the Ages*, pp. 104,114-115.
395) Orson Pratt, *The Seer*, p. 132.
396) Pratt, *The Seer*, p. 172; Stewart, *Brigham Young and His Wives*, p. 41.
397) Hunter, *Gospel Through the Ages*, p. 127; McConkie, *Mormon Doctrine*, pp. 589,750-751.

As Mormons we believed Jesus and Lucifer were spirit brothers, as well as spirit brothers to all mankind.[398]

I was taught that Lucifer presented his plan to be the savior of the world. Getting the glory for himself, he would redeem all mankind, without allowing one soul to be lost.[399] Jesus said he would give men their free agency of choice as on all other worlds before.

The council of the gods rejected Lucifer's plan and accepted Jesus' plan. Angered, Lucifer led a rebellion in heaven where he convinced one third of Elohim's spirit children to rebel with him.

He became Satan and was cast out. One third of the spirit children who rebelled with him became the demons and were sent to earth, where they were denied physical bodies forever.[400]

Mormon theology states that during this war in heaven, all the spirit children of Elohim who were unfaithful and not valiant came to earth cursed with black skin.[401] Those who were more noble were born into Mormon homes.[402] Therefore, I felt it was my reward from God to be born in these last days into a white Mormon home.

---

398) Hunter, *Gospel Through the Ages*, pp. 15,21; McConkie, *Mormon Doctrine*, pp. 192-193, 590.
399) Pearl of Great Price, Moses 4:1.
400) McConkie, *Mormon Doctrine,* pp. 193, 618.
401) *The Contributor,* vol. 6 pp. 296-297; Mark E. Peterson, *Race Problems— As They Affect The Church*, Address August 27, 1954; McConkie, *Mormon Doctrine*, p. 527.
402) *Journal of Discourses*, vol. 1 p. 63.

My Mormon Childhood Training

As a child, I would sit in my primary class and sing the songs, "I Am a Child of God" and "I Hope They Call Me on a Mission," hoping that someday I could fulfill a mission for the Mormon church.

At the age of eight, as with almost every Mormon boy or girl, I was baptized by immersion for the remission of sins[403] by my father, who, having the "proper authority," held the Melchizedek priesthood.

According to Mormonism, only Mormon men have been bestowed with the authority to baptize and marry. Their priesthood consists of two parts; the Aaronic and the Melchizedek.[404] I was then confirmed a member of the Church of Jesus Christ of Latter-day Saints.

Even as a child, I was eager to learn about the Mormon church, which I was told was the only true church upon the face of the earth.

Joseph Smith (the founder and first "prophet" of the LDS church) at the age of fourteen claimed to have wanted to know what denomination he should join, having heard of Methodist, Presbyterian, and Baptist faiths.

He went into the woods to pray. There he said he had a vision in which two personages he claimed were God the Father and Jesus Christ appeared to him and

---

403) LDS 4th Article of Faith; McConkie, *Mormon Doctrine*, p. 70.
404) Talmage, *Articles of Faith,* pp. 205-206; McConkie, *Mormon Doctrine*, p. 595.

told him he must join none of the Christian Churches for they were all wrong, their creeds were an abomination in God's sight and their professors were all corrupt.[405]

After he received this vision, he said an angel named Moroni visited him and told him where to find some gold plates. It was from these plates which he supposedly translated the Book of Mormon.[406]

Joseph Smith was also supposed to restore the church to the earth.[407] So on April 6, 1830, he started his church known as "The Church of Christ," later known as "The Church of the Latter Day Saints," now known as "The Church of Jesus Christ of Latter-day Saints."[408]

The early Mormon church leaders introduced several unique doctrines never before found in Orthodox Christianity. Their teachings included:

1. Polygamy: the practice of having more than one wife at the same time. They also taught that the god and Jesus Christ of Mormonism are polygamists.[409]

2. Blood atonement: the literal shedding of the blood of the sinner instead of relying on the shed blood of the Saviour, Jesus Christ.[410]

---

405) Pearl of Great Price, Joseph Smith History 1:1-20.
406) Ibid., 1:30-35; *Our Heritage*, published by the LDS church, p. 7.
407) *Our Heritage*, p. 4.
408) 1833 edition of the Book of Commandments (now known as the Doctrine and Covenants); 1835 edition of the Doctrine and Covenants 115:4.
409) Pratt, *The Seer*, p. 172; Stewart, *Brigham Young and His Wives*, p. 41.
410) Joseph Fielding Smith, *Doctrines of Salvation,* vol. 1, p. 134-135; *History of the Church*, vol. 5, p. 296; *Journal of Discourses* vol. 4, pp. 49-51, 53-54.

3. They also taught that there are millions of gods and that men may become a god.[411] One of my favorite sayings was, "As man is, God once was, as God is, man may become...[412]

After the Nauvoo Expositor exposed the teaching of the plurality of wives, Joseph Smith ordered the destruction of their printing press.[413] For this he was sentenced to the Carthage jail. While he was in jail a mob broke in and killed him.

I was taught that he was a martyr, that he sealed his testimony with his blood and that he said he was "led like a lamb to the slaughter...[414] I compared his death to the death of Jesus Christ on the cross. He was considered one of the saviors of mankind.[415]

But history proved that Joseph Smith did not go like a lamb to the slaughter. He shot three men; killing two and injuring the third in a gun battle before he was shot and killed.[416]

I was never taught that he killed anyone. I only learned the things that made him look wonderful. My teachers always seemed to leave out the facts, making him out to be more than just a mere human being. I placed

---

411) McConkie, *Mormon Doctrine*, pp. 613, 844; *Journal of Discourses* vol. 3, p. 93; Smith, *Teachings of the Prophet Joseph Smith*, p. 346.
412) Lorenzo Snow, Millennial Star, vol. 54, p. 404.
413) *History of the Church*, vol. 6, p. 432,448.
414) Doctrine and Covenants 135:4.
415) Ward Teachers Lesson for January, 1922.
416) *History of the Church*, vol. 6, pp. 617-618 and vol. 7, pp. 102-103.

him on a pedestal. He became the standard for what I wanted my husband to be, and his perfection was what I wished to achieve in my life.

I idolized Joseph Smith as the man God had chosen to bring the gospel and the church back to the earth. He was more important to me than Jesus Christ. When I attended the LDS church, our main focus was on Joseph Smith and what he had done for us. I was taught that if it had not been for him, there would have been no salvation.[417]

I was taught more about Joseph Smith and the Mormon "prophets" than any of the prophets in the Bible. Even during our monthly fast and testimony meetings, almost everyone's testimony would speak of their belief that the LDS church was true and that Joseph Smith was a true prophet. But seldom, if ever, were any praise or thanks given to the Lord for the sacrifice that Jesus Christ made on the cross for our sins.

I was taught that the Bible was the Word of God as far as it was translated correctly.[418] I didn't want to read the Bible, because I did not know which part I could trust. I believed that the Book of Mormon, Doctrine and Covenants and Pearl of Great Price were the only books I needed because Joseph Smith had written them, and I thought they were trustworthy.

---

417) McConkie, *Mormon Doctrine*, p. 670.
418) LDS 8th Article of Faith.

Polygamy Enters My Family

I was a sixth generation Mormon. My great, great, great grandfather, Milo Andrus, converted to Mormonism on March 12, 1832, just two years after the Mormon church began. He was acquainted with Joseph Smith and knew Brigham Young well. (Brigham Young later became the second "prophet" of the LDS church.)

My grandpa Milo was present when the official announcement about the doctrine and practice of plural marriage was made. Although he did not want to live as a polygamist, Brigham Young told him it was required of him. He eventually took plural wives at the expense of his marriage, as his first wife would not live polygamy. He had a total of eleven wives and fifty-seven children.[419]

My family all belonged to this "only true church." My father and mother were very devout Mormons. My dad was a member of the High Council. He and my mother saw to it that I attended church regularly, although I never had to be forced to go.

I thought the world of my parents. My dad was a truck driver, so I didn't get to see him very often. When he was home, he was either sleeping or reading. He had a set of the *Journal of Discourses* which contain the early Mormon teachings. This is what he read most of the time.

While reading these early LDS church writings, my dad's views started to change. He realized that the

---
419) Ivan J. Barrett, *Trumpeter of God*.

Mormon church of today is not what it was like in the beginning. Some of the doctrines, and even their stand on who God is, had changed.[420]

As a truck driver, my dad had several routes to southern Utah. This is where he met up with a group of Fundamentalist Mormons, who believe and practice the early teachings of Joseph Smith and Brigham Young, and still live polygamy. My dad studied with them as often as he could.

They expounded the early teachings and explained to my dad that they believed Wilford Woodruff, the fourth "prophet" of the LDS church, went astray by signing the Manifesto stopping polygamy.[421] Because of that, they had broken away from the mainstream Mormon church and formed their own church with their own "prophet." Yet they all still claim to be the "only true church."

After spending time with this group, and after a lot of personal study, my dad thought it was only right that he become a polygamist. Brigham Young taught that only those who enter into polygamy become gods.[422] Joseph Smith called polygamy the "New and Everlasting Covenant," and said all those who are not living it would be damned.[423]

---

420) Doctrine and Covenants 132; Official Declaration l; McConkie, *Mormon Doctrine*, p. 527; Official Declaration 2; *Journal of Discourses*, vol. 1, p. 50; Church News, Oct. 9, 1976.
421) Official Declaration l.
422) *Journal of Discourses*, vol. 11, p. 269.
423) Doctrine and Covenants 132:4,6.

While I was an 11-year-old child, my 53-year-old father brought home a 15-year-old girl and told us that he had to take her as his second wife in order to fulfill the law of eternal progression towards his own Godhood.

One day we were a happy family, and the next devastation struck our household. I thought she was my babysitter. Imagine my surprise when I learned she was going to be my "mother." I could not understand why my dad thought he needed another wife.

The Fruit of Polygamy Appears

I had never heard my parents argue—until that night. My mother cried as my father tried to get her to accept this girl into our home.

I laid in bed in fear, not knowing what the future would hold. I think my dad was surprised that my mother did not welcome this girl into our home with open arms. While it was a shock to the rest of us, he had already settled it in his mind that he must live polygamy. He had never told us of his secret meetings with this polygamist sect or of his findings as he studied the early Mormon doctrines.

Fear, hurt and anger hung over our house. My parents continued to fight, unable to settle their differences. And so, although I think my dad must have loved us, he left us to follow the early LDS teachings.

He went to live in Colorado City, Arizona, which is a polygamist community. My dad "married" this 15-year-old girl as his second wife and a short time later "married" her sister, having a total of three wives.

My mother was left alone to raise her seven children. I was the youngest. Three of us were still at home when he left. I am now the seventh of sixteen children, due to my dad's polygamist relationships.

My mother was hurt terribly and was very depressed after her husband left. After all, she had lived her life for him, and he had promised her everything—even eternity together.[424]

She was so devastated it was hard for her to function. She stayed on the couch, unable to go on. I got myself to and from school but when I came home, she would always be on the couch.

My sisters and I had to take on several responsibilities that were sometimes hard to handle. But through this ordeal, it was my mom who was hurt the most. Although she did not agree with my dad taking plural wives, she did not divorce him. She thought she still needed him because Mormons are taught that the men call their wives out of the grave and receive them into the celestial kingdom[425] (The highest level of the three degrees of the Mormon heavens).

I was still unsure why my dad thought he needed to "marry" other women. He said it was because he was

---

424) McConkie, *Mormon Doctrine*, pp.116-118.
425) *Journal of Discourses*, vol. 5, p. 291.

being a true Mormon. I thought I was a true Mormon, but I had never been taught in my ward (a local Mormon congregation) that I needed to live polygamy.

The Search For Truth Begins

I needed to find out for myself what had actually been taught on this subject so I could understand what had taken my dad away from me. I studied the Book of Mormon on my own, the book Joseph Smith said was the "most correct book on the earth."[426] Surely I would find my answers here, I thought.

I continued reading until I found what I was looking for. The Book of Mormon states that polygamy was abominable (Mosiah 11:2 and Jacob 2:24) and that God commanded man to have only one wife and no concubines (Jacob 2:27).

I was so excited! I had found something that would prove to my dad that what he was doing was wrong and he could come home. So I wrote him a letter with the verses I had found, hoping that shortly I would see him come back home.

One day he wrote back. He thanked me for writing and showing him those passages, but he said that he must live the true gospel by living polygamy. He pointed out that in the Doctrine and Covenants, another book written by Joseph Smith, polygamy is called the "new and ever-

---

426) *History of the Church*, vol. 4, p. 461.

lasting covenant…"[427] and he said it must be fulfilled. He told me it did not matter what was written in the Book of Mormon because other revelation revealed that polygamy was now commanded and good in the sight of the God of Mormonism.

He said I better live it also or I would be damned.[428] I wondered, "Where would I be damned to?" I had never heard about hell, and was never taught about a place of condemnation. I was taught that even the meanest sinner would find some place in the heavenly realm.[429]

I knew then that I had lost my father to a set of man-made doctrines and ungodly practices that even contradicted his own scriptures.

The Embarrassment of Polygamy

After my dad took plural wives, our lives took on a form of secrecy. I did not dare tell anyone where he had gone or what he had done. Polygamy was still illegal, although thousands were living it daily. I was afraid he would get arrested and be sent to jail.

I had to be very selective in the things I said. I became a very good liar, deceiving all those who asked me anything about him. Everything was a lie or a story. I never once felt any guilt for my actions because I thought I was protecting him.

---

427) Doctrine and Covenants 132:4,6.
428) Ibid. 132:4,6.
429) Joseph Smith, *Seeker After Truth*, pp. 177-178.

Some people knew what he had done and eventually most found out. We became outcasts. Even some of our friends became cold towards us. We were shunned by most of the members of our ward. I had a hard time understanding this. After all, my dad was only following Mormon doctrine, yet most of our friends and family were embarrassed by it.

Many Mormon people today are embarrassed by the doctrine of polygamy. Many even deny it was taught. But the fact is, it was taught, believed and lived.

Mormon doctrine states that polygamy is being lived by the "God" and "Jesus" of Mormonism and will be practiced throughout eternity by faithful Mormons. Mormon women who make it to the highest degree of heaven have only to look forward to sharing their husband with many other women for eternity.[430]

My "Burning in the Bosom"

Even at the young age of eleven, I began to see the contradictions and problems with the Mormon scriptures, but never once did I question the validity of the Mormon church. After all, from the time I could remember, I was told this was the only true church on the earth today. Why would I question it?

Seeing how polygamy had destroyed my family, I didn't like that particular doctrine, yet I still loved the Mormon church. I believed the LDS church was true, but

---

430) Pratt, *The Seer*, p. 37,39; Stewart, *Brigham Young and His Wives*, p. 41.

I knew it was time I got a "testimony" of its truthfulness for myself. I was taught that if I prayed about it, I could know by "a feeling" that the Mormon church and the Book of Mormon were true and that Joseph Smith was a true prophet.

So obeying the instructions I was given that if I asked God with a sincere heart if it was true, then I would receive my answer from the Holy Spirit. I knelt down and prayed, being assured that if I asked in faith, I would receive my answer. [431]

I then experienced having a "burning in my bosom." [432] This is a supernatural manifestation that Mormons teach is the Holy Ghost testifying to the truthfulness of Mormonism. It is interesting that in the Bible, Jesus says that when the Holy Spirit is come, He will testify of Jesus Christ, NOT a religious denomination (John 15:26).

I now had a testimony of my own. My belief that this was the only true church was even stronger than before.

My Zeal for Mormonism Grows

As I got older, my zeal to serve in the Mormon church continued to grow. When I was a teenager, I was able to go to the Salt Lake Temple to be baptized for the dead. Mormonism teaches that in order to get into the celestial kingdom, you must first be baptized into the Mormon church. For those who have died without a

---

431) Book of Mormon, Moroni 10:4.
432) Doctrine and Covenants 9:8.

Mormon baptism, someone has to stand in for them and be baptized by proxy.[433] This is the majority of the work performed in the LDS temples.

I looked forward to this with great anticipation. Before I was allowed into the temple, I had to be interviewed by my bishop. He asked me several questions about my commitment to the LDS church, if I had been paying my tithes, if I had been keeping the word of wisdom, which is abstinence from coffee, tea, alcohol, tobacco, drugs and caffeine.[434]

He also asked me several personal and embarrassing questions about my morality. Yet I sat facing him, looking him in the eyes, knowing that I could truthfully answer these questions because I had kept myself morally clean.

What a sobering occasion for me as I walked through the temple doors, knowing that I was one who was counted worthy to be doing work for the dead.[435] I was then baptized by immersion for about twenty to thirty dead people at a time.

When I was in the ninth grade, I took my first year of LDS seminary. Almost every public junior high and high school in the state of Utah has an LDS seminary building adjacent to the school where the students are allowed time to go learn Mormon doctrine.

---

433) McConkie, *Mormon Doctrine*, p. 73.
434) Ibid., p. 845
435) Smith, *Doctrines of Salvation*, vol. 2, pp. 146,149

I enjoyed this very much. During my sophomore, junior, and senior years, I also took seminary where I was in the class presidencies. This was a great opportunity to get trained in the Mormon teachings. I was also the president of my Mutual class.

One day during my seminary class, we had a guest speaker. He was dressed like a Catholic priest but we were told he was a Baptist preacher. He told our class that we needed to be saved by grace and quoted Ephesians 2:8-9 from the Bible:

> "For by grace are ye saved through faith; and that not of yourselves: it is the gift of God: Not of works, lest any man should boast."

This was the first time I had heard these verses. I jumped up and quoted a passage from the Book of Mormon:

> "…it is by grace that we are saved, after all we can do." (2 Nephi 25:23)

I told him that we have to do everything we can, and what we can't do, grace fills in. We had to work to get ourselves into heaven. The sacrifice that Jesus made on the cross was only for our physical resurrection.[436] If we wanted to get into the celestial kingdom we had to earn our own way.[437]

My class and I debated with him on the Mormon

---

436) McConkie, *Mormon Doctrine*, pp. 641, 669
437) Ibid., pp. 116-118.

teachings about salvation and exaltation into Godhood. After our discussion, he said that he could see that what we were saying was the truth and that he must be converted to Mormonism. I was commended for my excellent proselytizing tactics and told I would make a good missionary. This boosted my confidence in my religion and myself.

After class I found out the man was really a returned Mormon missionary, only playing the part to help train us. It didn't matter to me. I was happy knowing that I had succeeded in my first big lesson in converting someone to the LDS faith.

I loved my religion and was very self-righteous. I lived my religion to the fullest, loving the idea that my husband and I could someday be exalted to a god and a goddess in heaven, thinking that I was well on my way to accomplish this. I was very proud to be a Mormon and I thought very highly of myself.

There was no doubt in my mind that I would reach the celestial kingdom. I knew I had been living up to the standards set forth by the church. I attended our ward faithfully, paid my tithe and kept the word of wisdom. I was baptized for the dead and I dated only after the age of 16 and then it was only couple-dating. I was keeping myself morally clean so I could get married in the temple.

I knew I could achieve the goals I had set for myself. The only man I wanted to marry would be a returned Mormon missionary who was as righteous as I thought I was. We would go to the temple to be sealed together for eternity. Mormon doctrine claims that if a couple has a celestial or temple marriage they will be married throughout eternity and continue to procreate and fill their own world. Civil or marriages performed outside the temples are until death or divorce only.[438]

My desire was that my husband and I would continue to advance our positions of responsibility and prestige until eventually he would become the "prophet" and I would be the "prophet's wife." This was a position I knew I could fill. Throughout my life, I had been told I would be exalted, earning my own place in heaven, so I continued to work hard to insure my place in the highest level of heaven.

I Meet My Future Husband

When I was a senior in high school, I met my future husband. He was nothing like the man I had intended on marrying. In fact, he was just the opposite.

I met him one day when my Sunday school teacher (who was a returned Mormon missionary) was seen going into a house which was designated "off limits" to my girlfriends and me because boys who drank and did drugs partied there. We knew we needed to rescue our teacher, so my friends and I went up to the house. There we saw our teacher smoking and drinking. I couldn't believe it.

We were met by four other boys who were also

---

438) McConkie, *Mormon Doctrine*, pp. 117-118,146.

Mormon and three of them just happened to be in my ward. They were all smoking, drinking, and doing drugs. I assumed these guys just needed someone to get them back into the LDS church and I thought I was just the one to do it.

Richard was one of the boys who was drinking and doing drugs. I liked him instantly, but if I were to date him, he would have to conform to the standards of the Mormon church. I then made it my duty to try and mold him into the perfect Mormon man I wanted him to be.

My Fall into Sin Begins

My girlfriends and I continued to spend time with them until we all became very good friends. At first it was easy to resist the alcohol and drugs. But eventually my resistance wore down.

Several of my ward members accused me of doing things with these guys and this made me mad. Up to this point I had never drank, taken drugs or even kissed Richard. But slowly, my high moral standards started to decline. Instead of molding Richard into what I wanted him to be, he began reshaping me. I started to drink. Not much at first, but eventually I couldn't wait for the weekends so we could get drunk.

I finally graduated from high school and did not have to be under the watchful eye of my seminary teacher and classmates. I was sliding downhill fast. I didn't stop at alcohol; I also tried speed and cocaine. Richard and

I went to the bars to dance and drink. I knew I was no longer the righteous girl I once thought I was. My dreams and goals were quickly slipping out of my reach.

I started attending cosmetology school during the day and working at night. All the while, I was falling deeper in love with Richard. Occasionally he would go to our ward with me, when his hangovers weren't too bad, which wasn't very often.

I had stopped the drugs, but was still drinking. I kept falling deeper into sin, although I never realized I was sinning against God. I only thought I was being disobedient to the Mormon church.

"Oh no... I'm Pregnant"

I eventually found out I was pregnant. My life became unbearable. Several people in my ward turned their back on me. Others could only say, "I told you so." Some were nice, but not very many.

Richard and I had been engaged for over a year and I thought our getting married would help bring back some of the respect I wished for. But we had been having some problems. I was stubborn and still wanted my temple marriage, and I blamed Richard for all of my failed dreams.

Richard disliked me for making him feel like he was being trapped into marriage, and I resented him for everything that had happened to me. Because of this, we did not get married. Here I was, an unwed, pregnant

Mormon girl. This was not how my life was supposed to turn out. How could this have happened to me?

I finished cosmetology school but I no longer wanted to do hair, so I got a job in a day care. My heart broke as I took care of children who came from broken homes because I knew my own child was facing this same fate.

Richard and I saw each other once in a while, but our families didn't make it any easier on us. Mine disliked him, his disliked me. I cried myself to sleep night after night; hating the circumstances which had brought me to this deep despair. I only attended my ward once in a while now. I could not stand to see everyone's looks of pity and disappointment.

Finally, I had my baby. While I was in the hospital before she was born, how I wished Richard and I had been married, but it didn't happen. We had a beautiful little girl and I was a single mother. Fear gripped my heart as I wondered how I could take care of her.

My family was very good to me during this time. They helped me and gave me all the love and support I needed. But it wasn't enough. I wanted a husband and wanted my daughter to know her father.

Richard was buying his own home so I moved in with him. He was a good father but our living together did not solve any of our problems; it only made them worse. I had stopped drinking when I found out I was pregnant and was now trying to pull my life together.

Life was miserable for all of us. I had sunk so low into sin that I could hardly stand myself. Long gone were the days when I considered myself good enough to be a Goddess over my own world.

Getting Married Doesn't Help

Richard and I knew something needed to be done about our situation, so we got married. I wanted a big, beautiful wedding but we just appeared before a Justice of the Peace. Richard had gone to a party the night before we got married and got so drunk that he barely arrived at the courthouse that morning because he had a hangover.

Once again, this was nothing like I had envisioned for myself. It was awful. A few of our family members came but the day turned out to be a big disappointment for me. No beautiful dress, no bridesmaids, no walking down the aisle, no celebration, nothing fancy; just simply saying "I do" to a man who could barely stand up.

Life together was still terrible when I found out I was pregnant again. Richard and I still didn't like each other very much but we were trying to make things work.

Richard Starts Attacking My Religion

While I was about five months along, Richard's life started to change. He stopped doing drugs and drinking. As soon as he came home from work he didn't run to the refrigerator for a beer. Instead he would say to me, "God loves you." This was not like him.

My husband, who used to care more about getting his next drink, was now telling me that God loved me.

I started thinking that maybe he was finally willing to take me to the temple, where our family could be sealed together forever. I thought all of my work in trying to get him to be a good Mormon was finally paying off.

But one day when Richard came home from work, he said something that altered the course of my life forever. He said:

> "Cindy, the Mormon church is not true, I cannot stay in it and I want you out of it, too."

Never had anyone spoken such hurtful words to me. The mere thought that my church might not be true outraged me. Who did he think he was to say this to me? How dare he utter such words to me after he had crushed all of my dreams and ruined my life?

Life in our house became worse. Everyday when Richard came home from work, he wanted to talk about the Mormon teachings. He would ask me questions about the early LDS doctrines I had never heard of, such as:

• The Jesus of Mormonism was not conceived by the Holy Ghost or born of a virgin, but was conceived by a physical relationship between the god of Mormonism and his spiritual daughter Mary.[439]

---

439) *Journal of Discourses* vol. 8, p. 115; Smith, *Doctrines of Salvation*, vol. 1, p. 18; Hunter, *The Gospel Through the Ages*, p. 120.

- Joseph Smith had several "first" visions[440] and that his prophecies had failed.[441]

I was irrational, only responding with my testimony of the truthfulness of the LDS church. I did not have any answers as to why the doctrines had been changed or why almost 4,000 changes had been made to the Book of Mormon since it first came out in 1830.[442]

I was confused as to why the Book of Mormon, which is supposedly the "most correct" book on the earth, does not contain the major doctrines of the Mormon church.

I could not answer why the Mormon church does not use the Inspired Version of the Bible that Joseph Smith wrote.

All I could tell him was that he needed to talk to the Mormon missionaries, as I was not as smart as them. How could the LDS church not be true? After all, it contained the name of Jesus Christ right in its title.

Everyday was the same thing. I couldn't wait for Richard to leave the house for work so I could be left alone. It would have been fine with me if he had never come home. But each night he did, and it was always the same thing — more talk and more Mormon questions.

Everyday Richard would bring me home literature

---

440) Colleen Raison, *The First Vision Quilt*.
441) *History of the Church*, vol. 2, p. 182; Oliver B. Huntington Journal, book 14; Doctrine and Covenants 84:1-5; Whitmer, *An Address To All Believers In Christ*, pp. 30-31.
442) Tanner, *3,913 Changes in the Book of Mormon*.

about problems with Mormon teachings. I was so angry. I told him it was all anti-Mormon literature, but I never took the time to notice that it was all taken straight out of LDS sources.

Biblical Gospel tracts were dispersed throughout our home so I would find them. He brought movies home for me to watch and tapes for me to listen to. I was going crazy. I could not stand it anymore. I was angry at him all the time. I did not want to live like this any longer.

But the most remarkable thing that occurred during this time was the change in Richard. Even though I hated him and was so angry at him, I could see how he was changing. He no longer listened to rock music, he stopped cursing, his want for alcohol ceased and he had a genuine love for our family. He was no longer angry all the time. He was a different person.

Richard had been working with a man who was a Christian, and this man had been showing Richard the changes in the LDS teachings and talking to him about the Bible and the Jesus Christ of the Bible. Richard had realized his need for the Saviour. He had stopped trusting in himself and his religion and had received the Lord Jesus Christ into his heart and life as his personal Saviour and had become a born again Christian.

But still I hated my husband. Life with him was terrible. I had just had our second child, another beautiful little girl, when I decided I couldn't live like this any more. I was so angry with Richard for telling me the

Mormon church was not true. After all, he had been raised Mormon all of his life, too.

Some of the leaders of our ward came to our house and counseled me to leave him and find a faithful Mormon who would take me to the temple. I decided this would be the best thing for everyone involved. I found a divorce lawyer and was going to end this marriage.

The only vehicle we had was a truck with a stick shift which I had a hard time driving. I sat in that truck with the lawyer's address in my hand, ready to go, but I couldn't put the truck in reverse to get out of the driveway. I was furious.

My New Plan to Defend Mormonism

I was so angry that the only thought that came to my mind was that I could not leave with Richard thinking he was right. I had to prove to him that the Mormon church was true. Then he would have to apologize to me for all those months of misery.

A new plan started to form in my mind. Since I couldn't leave, I would find the answers to all of the questions he had asked and show him that I was right and he was wrong.

I went to the library and checked out every book I could find on the early LDS church history and doctrines. I studied during all of my spare time, trying to find something that would support my claims.

The more I studied, the more I realized how little

I really knew about my religion. Instead of finding the answers I was looking for, I found more questions and problems. I saw how some of the major doctrines had been changed.

• When polygamy was given it was essential to salvation.[443] Now it was no longer required.[444]

• At one time, Adam was the god of Mormonism. (This was called scripture by Brigham Young.[445]) Then Spencer W. Kimball, the twelfth "prophet" of the LDS church called it false doctrine.[446]

• Black people were once called an inferior race[447] and told they were unworthy and unable to hold the Mormon priesthood.[448] Yet on June 9, 1978, in the Deseret News, Spencer W. Kimball announced that by "revelation" black people could now hold the Mormon priesthood.[449]

Although my dad, after studying the early church doctrines, became a polygamist, I did not know what I should do. Which "prophet" should I follow?

I read many prophecies that Joseph Smith made that did not come to pass. One really scared me. Joseph Smith gave a revelation that the copyright of the Book of

---

443) Doctrine and Covenants 132:4; *Journal of Discourses*, vol. 20, p. 28.
444) Official Declaration 1.
445) *Journal of Discourses*, vol. 1, pp. 50-51; vol. 13, p. 95.
446) Church News, October 9, 1976.
447) Smith, *The Way To Perfection*, pp. 101-102.
448) McConkie, *Mormon Doctrine*, p. 527.
449) Also found in the Official Declaration 2.

Mormon would be sold in Canada. But after his prophecy failed completely, his explanation was, "Some revelations are of God: some revelations are of man: and some revelations are of the devil."[450]

It scared me thinking that I was trusting my eternal existence on someone who did not even know who his revelations were coming from.

I read how the blood atonement doctrine was put into actual practice, and how people lost their lives by having their throat slit from ear to ear to allow their blood to be spilt to atone for their sins.[451]

And in the temple ceremony, all those who participate make oaths to remind themselves of what will happen to them if they ever reveal the secrets that are performed in there.

During one part of the temple ceremony, a man portraying Lucifer reveals that the green fig leaf apron is an emblem of his power and priesthoods, and he instructs everyone to place one around their waist.[452]

I read about Joseph Smith's claim of "knowing more than all the world put together,"[453] and his boasting of doing greater things than Jesus.[454]

I learned how he was involved in the occult by using

---

450) Whitmer, *An Address To All Believers In Christ*, pp. 30-31.
451) Confessions of John D. Lee, 1880, pp. 282-283.
452) Chuck Sackett, *What's Going On In There?*
453) *Journal of Discourses*, vol. 6, p. 5.
454) History of the Church, vol. 6, pp. 408-409.

divining rods and claiming to use a seer stone in translating the Book of Mormon.[455]

However, the thing that scared me the most was when I realized, after I really started to read the Christian Gospel tracts and my Bible, that the Mormon church's teachings and the Bible do not go hand in hand like I had been taught. In fact, Mormonism was in direct opposition to what the God of the Bible has spoken.

My Doubts About Mormonism Begin

I did not dare tell Richard of my discoveries just yet. I was scared. What was I trusting in for my eternal life? I did not know what to believe.

One day while Richard was at work, I got out one of the papers he had brought home for me to read. It had a picture of a Christian missionary family who had given their lives (not just two years) to serve God. They gave their testimony about their love and gratitude for Jesus, thanking Him for saving their souls. Their love for the Saviour was so real and genuine.

My heart longed to know this Jesus they were speaking about. The only "Jesus" I knew about was just my brother and example, and I could be just as good as him if I tried.

As a Mormon, I never gave my worship and adoration to the Lord. All of my love and devotion went to Joseph

---

455) Book of Commandments 7:3 (now known as the Doctrine and Covenants); Whitmer, *An Address To All Believers In Christ*, p. 12.

Smith and the Mormon church. But now I wanted to know this Jesus who could save my soul.

During this time of my research, Richard's and my life was still horrible. Richard was changing, getting kinder and happier all the time. I was getting angrier, still trying to hold onto the belief that the Mormon church was true. I thought maybe the problems were with the people and not the LDS church itself. But the more I studied, the more I realized there were too many contradictions and changes for it to be true.

Richard had been speaking to his co-worker about a subject I had never heard of; it was called the "Rapture," which is described in 1 Thessalonians 4:16-17:

> "For the Lord himself shall descend from heaven with a shout, with the voice of the archangel, and with the trump of God: and the dead in Christ shall rise first: Then we which are alive and remain shall be caught up together with them in the clouds, to meet the Lord in the air: and so shall we ever be with the Lord."

One day when Richard came home from work, he told me the most frightening words I had ever heard. He said:

> "When the Rapture occurs, me and our two girls will be gone but you will be left behind."

Not only did this scare me, but it confused me. I had never heard about the Rapture. And who was Richard to say I could not go? I had always lived a better life than he had. Surely I could go.

I was still so angry at Richard it would not have mattered to me where he went, but I did not want my daughters going anywhere without me. Even though I did not believe what he had said, I was scared. I did not want to be left behind.

All of my life I had been taught that the Mormon church was the only true church. But I knew I needed to seriously reconsider what I was basing my eternal life on. I wanted what that Christian missionary family and Richard had. Richard's life had been completely changed and I knew it was not a religion that had made the difference. He was not even attending any church at the time. It was a personal relationship with the Jesus Christ of the Bible.

I Finally Get Saved

While I was searching for the answers I so desperately wanted, I picked up a book from our bookshelf titled, *God's Word: Final, Infallible and Forever*. Our Christian neighbor up the street had left it on our doorstep during an outreach in our area about one year prior to this. The only reason Richard kept it was because it had a nice landscape cover. This book was written to show the validity of the Bible as the Word of God, as well as some of the problems with the Mormon teachings.

The first section told about the Bible being the only

Word of God and explained how the God of the Bible is All Powerful and is able to keep His Word pure for us today in the King James Version.[456]

I learned that the Bible is trustworthy and has no errors. I had never heard this before, as I had always been taught that the Bible had been mistranslated,[457] and that many plain and precious parts were taken out.[458] I was very excited as I thought about there being a God who is powerful enough to preserve His Word for me.

The next section told of some of the problems in the Mormon teachings. These were some of the things I had already been studying and this reinforced my doubts. There was also a Biblical plan of salvation. It was so wonderful and simple that I thought it was too easy. How could I just believe on and receive Jesus Christ for my salvation?

I remembered the verses quoted to me by the man who pretended to be a Baptist preacher from my seminary class (Ephesians 2:8-9). I knew if I could get to heaven on my own, then I would boast for all eternity about all the good works I had done to get myself there and that would be unacceptable to God. I didn't want to trust my way anymore; I wanted God's way.

First, I had to realize I was a sinner. The Bible says, "As it is written, There is none righteous, no, not one"

---

456) Matthew 24:35, Psalm 12:6-7, 2 Timothy 3:16, 1 Peter 1:23-25.
457) LDS 8th Article of Faith.
458) Book of Mormon, 1 Nephi 13:26.

(Romans 3:10). "For all have sinned and come short of the glory of God" (Romans 3:23).

Before I met Richard, I never thought I had sinned. I was the epitome of perfection in my own mind. But after we met, I did drugs, drank, ended up an unwed mother and was angry all the time.

Yes, I now knew I was a sinner. I had been brought down to the lowest point in my life. I had sinned against a holy and righteous God.

Next, the Bible said there was a penalty for my sin—a burning lake of fire forever. "For the wages of sin is death…" (Romans 6:23a). "And death and hell were cast into the lake of fire. This is the second death" (Revelation 20:14).

> "But the fearful, and unbelieving, and the abominable, and murderers, and whoremongers, and sorcerers, and idolaters, and all liars, shall have their part in the lake which burneth with fire and brimstone: which is the second death." (Revelation 21:8)

Well, I had never heard this but I knew I deserved it because I had sinned. The Bible said that Jesus died to pay for my sin. When he died on that old, cruel cross two thousand years ago, my sins were placed on Him. Jesus died so I might live:

> "But God commendeth his love toward us, in that, while we were yet sinners, Christ died for us." (Romans 5:8)

I had always heard that Jesus died for me, but that, I was told, was only for my physical resurrection. To get myself into heaven, I had to work. Then I wondered, "How much work would it take?" Even if I repented and went back to the LDS church faithfully, went through the temple, paid my tithe and did my work for the dead, would it be enough? How would I know when I had done all I needed to do?

I wondered if, when I died and stood before God, He would say I was $1.00 short on my tithe or I missed one week too many of church to get into the degree of heaven I desired to attain. How would I know?

The Jesus of the Bible died not only for my physical resurrection but also for the salvation of my spirit and soul. He is able to forgive all of my sins and save me:

> "Wherefore he is able also to save them to the uttermost that come unto God by him..." (Hebrews 7:25)

As a Mormon, I was taught that baptism washed away my sins, and I was baptized at the age of eight. Can you imagine all of the sins I had accumulated since then?

Mormon doctrine also states that once I repented, if I sinned again, every previous sin would come back.[459] This was terrible. If God would not allow sin into His Heaven, then I would not be allowed in.

I never knew that I was a sinner in need of a Saviour.

---

459) Doctrine and Covenants 82:7; Kimball, *Miracle of Forgiveness*, p. 170.

I thought I could get into heaven on my own merit. But Jesus said:

> "...I am the way, the truth, and the life: no man cometh unto the Father, but by me."
> (John 14:6)

I finally started to understand that only Jesus could get me into heaven, not my church, my water baptism, or all of the wonderful good works I could perform. I learned from the Bible that:

> "...all our righteousnesses are as filthy rags..." (Isaiah 64:6)

> "Not by works of righteousness which we have done, but according to his mercy he saved us..." (Titus 3:5)

I also began to see that only by the blood of Jesus Christ can we have forgiveness of sin:

> "...Unto him that loved us, and washed us from our sins in his own blood..."
> (Revelation 1:5)

Unlike my religion, the Bible said salvation is a gift from God:

> "...the gift of God is eternal life through Jesus Christ our Lord." (Romans 6:23b)

I knew that a gift is something I did not have to work for, only acknowledge it was being offered and receive it.

I finally realized I was a sinner, and I recognized the penalty for my sin. I understood that I could not get myself into heaven. I saw that, by faith, I needed to trust Jesus Christ alone, plus and minus nothing, and ask Him to forgive me and save me:

> "That if thou shalt confess with thy mouth the Lord Jesus, and shalt believe in thine heart that God hath raised him from the dead, thou shalt be saved. For with the heart man believeth unto righteousness; and with the mouth confession is made unto salvation." (Romans 10:9-10)

> "For whosoever shall call upon the name of the Lord shall be saved." (Romans 10:13)

I now knew that my religion could never get me into heaven.

In the book I was reading, after the Biblical plan of Salvation, there was a sinner's prayer. I went into my bedroom and knelt down by my bed and simply read the prayer as it was written in the book:

> "Lord Jesus Christ, come into my heart and life. Cleanse me from all my sin by your shed blood. Make me a child of God. Give me your free gift of everlasting life, and let me know I am saved, now and forever. I now receive you as my very own personal Saviour, in Jesus' name, Amen."

As soon as I asked the Jesus Christ of the Bible to forgive me and come into my heart and life and save me, my life was changed forever.

I then realized I had been wandering around in spiritual darkness all of my life. But when I trusted Jesus Christ alone as my Saviour, my eyes were opened and I could see. I came out of the darkness and into His marvelous light (1 Peter 2:9).

I knew at that moment that everything I had been raised with and had been trusting in for my eternal life was wrong. I realized that no religion could get me into heaven—only a relationship with Jesus Christ could do that.

My New Life In Christ Begins

My life had been changed in a moment. I now had a personal relationship with the living Lord, Jesus Christ. I had been forgiven, saved and born again into God's family, becoming His child (John 1:12, Ephesians 1:5). I knew salvation was instantaneous and not a process of works (Romans 6:23, Ephesians 2:8-9).

I had to tell someone, so I told Richard. I had to admit to him that I had been wrong, but that didn't matter. I now had peace and I knew for certain where I would go if the rapture occurred or when I died. I would be in heaven with Jesus, not because of anything that I had done, but because of everything that Jesus had done for me on the cross.

By the grace of God, Richard and I started rebuilding our life together. It was only by that grace that we are still married because of the bitterness and resentment we had for each other. It has taken time, but God has restored our love for each other and has even given me a greater love and deeper respect for my husband.

Rejected by our Families

We knew it was time to tell our families that we were no longer attending the LDS church. We hoped they would be happy that someone was finally sharing the truth with them from the Bible.

Were we ever wrong! They had the same reaction with us that I had with Richard—anger, resentment and unbelief. Our families couldn't understand how we could do this to them.

The closest Richard has ever come to being physically assaulted for the cause of Christ was from his own family. Our relationship with them has never been the same. Some of them wanted nothing to do with us.

Our hearts break for our friends and family because we know the bondage they are under, trying to live up to the expectations of thinking they can become a god. It cannot be done. There is only one God and no one will ever become one.[460]

In Genesis chapter 3 in the Bible, we learn that it was Satan who first introduced the doctrine that man could become as god:

---

460) Deuteronomy 4:35,39; 6:4, Isaiah 43:10-11; 44:6,8; 45:5-6,18,21-22; 46:9, Psalm 86:10, Mark 12:29,32; 1 Timothy 2:5, 1 John 5:7.

> "And the serpent said unto the woman, Ye shall not surely die: For God doth know that in the day ye eat thereof, then your eyes shall be opened, and ye shall be as gods…"

This is Satan's number one doctrine. It was because of this belief that Satan was cast out of heaven (Isaiah 14:12-15). All creation was cursed because of the fall of man. It was not a fall upward, as Mormonism teaches.[461]

We Are Not Attacking — We Are Defending

Please understand that we are not attacking anyone. Jude 3 tells us to "earnestly contend for the faith which was once delivered unto the saints." We are defending the Lord Jesus Christ's claim that He established His Church, and His promise to keep and preserve it.

> "And I say also unto thee, That thou art Peter, and upon this rock I will build my church; and the gates of hell shall not prevail against it." (Matthew 16:18)[462]

The LDS church was started because Joseph Smith claimed that all Christian Churches were wrong, their creeds were an abomination in God's sight and their professors were all corrupt.[463]

Joseph Smith said the Church that Jesus Christ started

---
461) Sterling W. Sill, Deseret News, Church Section, July 31, 1965, p. 7.; Joseph Fielding Smith, *Answers to Gospel Questions*, p. 60; Smith, *Doctrines of Salvation*, vol. 1, pp. 114-115.
462) See 1 Corinthians 3:11, Ephesians 2:20, Acts 2:47, Jude 3, 1 Peter 1:25.
463) Pearl of Great Price, Joseph Smith History 1:19.

and promised to preserve had gone into apostasy, and he was called to restore it.[464]

The Lord Jesus Christ said not even the gates of hell would prevail against His Church.

Which One Will You Believe?

"And if it seem evil unto you to serve the LORD, choose you this day whom ye will serve; whether the gods which your fathers served that were on the other side of the flood, or the gods of the Amorites, in whose land ye dwell: but as for me and my house, we will serve the LORD." (Joshua 24:15)

---

464) McConkie, *Mormon Doctrine*, pp. 136-137; *Our Heritage*, p. 4.

SUMMARY OF WHAT MORMONS BELIEVE

BEGINNINGS: HOW MORMONS BELIEVE IT ALL BEGAN

1. We all existed as spirit children of God the Father in heaven before we were born on earth.[465]

2. Our Father in heaven deemed it necessary for his children to further their education and experience.[466]

3. He called a council in heaven of all the gods and leading spirits.[467]

4. Options were offered on how this new experience would be conducted.[468]

5. Lucifer, one of God the Father's spirit children, offered to be the savior of all mankind and save everyone.

6. Jesus, God the Father's oldest spirit child, offered to be the savior of mankind and allow all to have the

---

465) Pearl of Great Price, Abraham 3:22.
466) Doctrines of Salvation, vol. 1, pp. 56-57.
467) Joseph Fielding Smith, *Teachings of the Prophet Joseph Smith,* p. 349.
468) Pearl of Great Price, Moses 4:1-4.

freedom to choose to follow God's plan for salvation and future exaltation, as they had done on past worlds.[469]

7. Jesus' plan was accepted, Lucifer's was rejected. Lucifer then led a rebellion in heaven, convincing one third of his spirit brothers and sisters to rebel against God the Father. Lucifer became the devil and those who followed him became the demons.[470]

8. After losing a battle in heaven, Lucifer and the demons were cast out. The spirit children who fought valiantly in heaven were born to white, LDS families. The spirit children who did not fight were cursed with the mark of Cain, to be born into families with dark skin.[471]

9. Adam and Eve were placed in the Garden of Eden and were given conflicting commandments: not to eat of the tree of the knowledge of good and evil, or to multiply and replenish the earth.[472] They took of the fruit and were cast out of the garden, which was a fall upward towards salvation and exaltation.[473]

10. Adam was baptized and then he received the Holy Spirit after the Lord had revealed to Adam that he was forgiven of all his sins. He received the priesthood and became the first patriarch on the earth.[474]

---

469) *Journal of Discourses*, vol. 6, p. 8.
470) Doctrine and Covenants 29:36-38.
471) Mormon Doctrine, pp. 526-527.
472) Book of Mormon, 2 Nephi 2:22-23, 25.
473) Pearl of Great Price, Moses 5:10-11.
474) Moses 5:9, 6:52, 64-65.

HOW MORMONS BELIEVE THEY CAME TO AMERICA

11. Jared and the Jaredites (later known as the Lamanites, believed to be the American Indian descendents) came to America on ships.[475]

12. The Nephites came from Jerusalem to South America about 600 B.C.[476]

13. The Nephites' wickedness even surpassed that of their brothers, the Lamanites (American Indians). The Lord allowed the Lamanites to annihilate all the Nephites except Moroni. He was commanded by the Lord to bury the record of his people on golden plates (known today as the Book of Mormon) in the hill Cumorah.[477]

HOW MORMONISM STARTED WITH JOSEPH SMITH

14. Fourteen hundred years after Moroni buried the golden plates, he appeared as an angel to Joseph Smith and directed him where to find them.[478]

15. Joseph Smith, at age fourteen, said that God the Father and Jesus Christ appeared to him and told him not to join any Christian Church, as all were an abomination; all the workers were corrupt and the Church that Jesus Christ had established had gone into complete apostasy.[479]

---

475) Ether 2:24, 6:5-11.
476) 1 Nephi 18:23-25.
477) Mormon 6.
478) Pearl of Great Price, Joseph Smith History 1:30-35.
479) Ibid. 1:1-20.

16. Joseph Smith was given the responsibility to restore the church and translate the golden plates to English from reformed Egyptian.[480]

17. The LDS church, first known as the Church of Christ, later The Church of the Latter Day Saints, now known as The Church of Jesus Christ of Latter-day Saints was started on April 6th, 1830, with 6 members.[481]

18. Joseph Smith was killed in a gun battle while being held in the Carthage jail for ordering the destruction of the printing press that exposed his teachings on polygamy and plurality of Gods.[482]

19. Brigham Young, second president and prophet of the Mormon church, led a majority of LDS followers to Salt Lake City, Utah in 1847.

20. The Manifesto was signed, denouncing the practice of polygamy by the LDS church, yet still considered an eternal and unchangeable doctrine for godhood.[483]

21. The doctrine banning dark skinned races to hold the Mormon priesthood changed.[484]

22. Today, Thomas S. Monson, 16th President and prophet of the LDS church presides over 14 million members, with 60,000 Mormon missionaries around the world, and 40,000 more home missionaries.

---

480) Our Heritage, pp. 4,7.
481) Doctrine and Covenants 20:1.
482) History of the Church, vol. 6, pp. 432,448.
483) Official Declaration-1; Doctrine and Covenants 132.
484) Official Declaration-2; Mormon Doctrine, p. 527.

ARE MORMONS ENCOURAGED TO LIE?

Now that you have all of this knowledge about Mormon doctrine, there is one more important practice you need to be aware of before you go out and start talking to Mormons about their religion.

You need to know that under certain circumstances, Mormons are not only allowed, but encouraged, to lie right to your face.

For example, if lying will help protect the LDS church, they are encouraged to do so.

Or if it will help recruit you into their religion, lying to you is permitted. They call it, "Lying for the Lord."

> "For the Mormon, loyalty and the welfare of the church are more important than the principle of honesty, and plausible denials and deception by omission are warranted by an opportunity to have the Mormon organization seen in the best possible light."[485]

> "And whatsoever thing persuadeth men to do good is of me;"[486]

---
485) www.mormonwiki.org/Lying_for_the_Lord
486) Book of Mormon, Ether 4:12

Let's say you are talking to a Mormon and you say, "I heard that your religion believes that men can become gods."

You continue, "I can't believe your religion really teaches something that bizarre. Is it true?"

Since the Mormon detects that this belief offends you and could stop you from becoming a member, he or she is authorized to say, "Absolutely not. Our religion has never taught that."

Then, once you are incorporated into the church, and you learn the truth, they will tell you they couldn't tell you back then because you simply weren't ready for it. They justify it by calling it "Milk before meat."

But no matter what they call it, it's still lying.

So when you go out and begin asking Mormons about their strange doctrines, don't be surprised if they deny everything. That's what they've been taught to do. To them, it's a good thing to lie … as long as it's "for the Lord."

Of course, you can't assume they are always lying. Some Mormons might honestly not know some of the more bizarre doctrines of their religion. So give them the benefit of the doubt and show them the facts before assuming they are lying.

CONCLUSION

Are you a Mormon?

If so, we pray that the facts in this book have shown you how dramatically (and often) the doctrines of your religion contradict the Bible. And we pray that you are now open to the possibility that the following verse from the Bible applies to you:

> "In whom the god of this world hath blinded the minds of them which believe not, lest the light of the glorious gospel of Christ, who is the image of God, should shine unto them."
> (2 Corinthians 4:4)

It's true. The reason you have believed all these unbiblical Mormon doctrines and rejected the true gospel of salvation by faith alone in Jesus Christ is because Satan has blinded your mind.

But now you have seen the facts. Now you know that Joseph Smith was nothing more than a con man. And you are aware that many Mormon doctrines directly contradict God's holy Word.

Knowing all this, we urge you to reject the Mormon religion, and all its false teachings. We pray that you will trust the Lord Jesus Christ for your salvation by accepting

Him as your personal Saviour and receive His free gift of eternal life.

Are you a Christian?

If so, our prayer is that you are now more motivated and better equipped to share the gospel with these lost religious people.

And we pray that you will use this knowledge that God has given you to lovingly show Mormons the errors of their religion, and to present to them the true gospel of salvation by faith alone through Jesus Christ.

May God richly bless you.

Made in the USA
Columbia, SC
02 August 2023